W.B. YEATS

GREENWICH EXCHANGE
LONDON

The Poetry of
W.B. YEATS

John Greening

Greenwich Exchange, London

First published in Great Britain in 2005
Reprinted 2011

Printed and bound by imprintdigital.net
Cover design by December Publications
Tel: 028 90286559
Cover image of W.B. Yeats
courtesy of Mary Evans Picture Library

Greenwich Exchange Website: www.greenex.co.uk

Cataloguing in Publication Data is available
from the British Library

ISBN: 978-1-871551-34-1

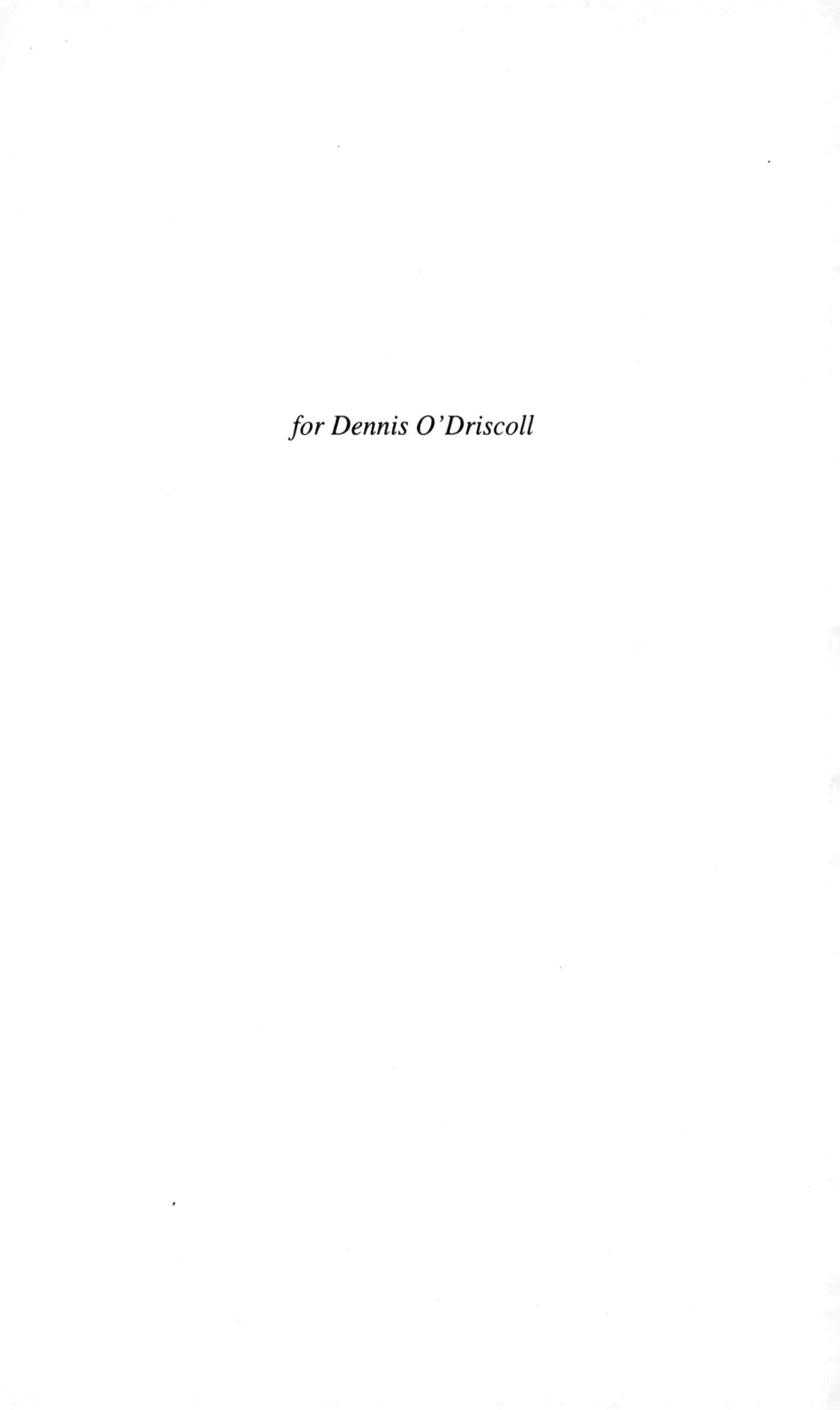

for Dennis O'Driscoll

“I am still of the opinion that only two topics can
be of the least interest to a serious and
studious mind – sex & the dead.”

W.B. Yeats: letter to Olivia Shakespear, October 1927

Contents

Prefatory Note

O chestnut-tree, great-rooted blossomer,
Are you the leaf, the blossom or the bole?

To write about William Butler Yeats is to be faced with several men at once: the dramatist, essayist, spiritualist, revolutionary, theatre manager, senator, socialite, lover, friend ... It is not surprising that the most recent biography (R.F. Foster's) runs to two substantial volumes and that every month seems to see a new book about him. But the 'bole' of the man is Yeats the poet and this particular book is about his poetry. The chapters are arranged thematically, although there is the shadow of a chronology since the mythological and love poems tended to come first, then the political ones, then the occult and so on. I have not attempted to tackle the plays, except where relevant to the poetry. Nor have I explored the long poems and dramatic dialogues in any detail. The essays, fairytales, the one novel and *A Vision* only receive passing mention. My aim was to remind readers why we should continue to read Yeats and to explain what it is in the craftsmanship of his verse that makes it so original and enduring. I suggest that this book is read in conjunction with one of the biographies (Roy Foster's landmark twin volumes, *The Apprentice Mage* and *The Arch-Poet* or Stephen Coote's excellent and compact *Life*) and with a copy of the *Collected Poems* to hand. I worked from Richard J. Finneran's 1989 edition of *The Poems*, but there are many useful annotated compilations: from Dent, edited by Daniel Albright, for example (1994), and Norman Jeffares' extensive (and thematically arranged) 1988 selection from Macmillan. Indeed, for all the academic flurry of publications in the last decade, there is little wrong with the old original Macmillan 'definitive' *Collected.*

Chronology

1865 13th June, Yeats born Sandymount Avenue, Dublin. Eldest child of John and Susan. Siblings: Lily (1866), Lolly (1868), Jack (1871).

1867 To Regent's Park, London (house in which Sylvia Plath would almost a century later commit suicide), later Fulham, finally Bedford Park. Yeats taught by father, then at Godolphin School, Hammersmith. Holidays at Sligo on west coast of Ireland with mother's family, the Pollexfens.

1871 J.M. Synge born.

1881 Yeats family returns to Ireland: Howth. Parnell imprisoned.

1882 Writes first poems.

1884 Metropolitan School of Art, Dublin – not Trinity College, which his father J.B. would have preferred. Meets George Russell ('AE'). Falls in love with cousin.

1885 Family moves into Dublin. Early lyrics published. Involved with Dublin Hermetic/Theosophical Society. Friendship with Katharine Tynan and old Fenian, O'Leary. Writes 'Song of the Happy Shepherd'. Ezra Pound born.

1886 Abandons art. Attends séances. Writes 'The Stolen Child'. Home Rule Bill defeated.

1887-8 Family move to London again: Bedford Park. Mother has two strokes. Interest in theosophy. Meets wider literary circle – Wilde, Henley, Morris. Attends séance that terrifies him. Completes 'Down by the Salley Gardens' and his long poem 'The Wanderings of Oisin'. Reputation is building.

Commissioned to write fairytale book. *Poems and Ballads of Young Ireland* appears.

1889 Meets Maud Gonne, who calls at his home in Bedford Park. First collection, *The Wanderings of Oisin and Other Poems*. Begins editing Blake edition. Writes poems which will appear later as *Crossways*. Writes play, *The Countess Cathleen*.

1890 Completes 'The Lake Isle of Innisfree', which he will come to detest. Meets Florence Farr. Occult interests. Initiated into the Order of the Golden Dawn.

1891 Proposes to Maud Gonne. Death of her son, whom Yeats believed to be adopted. He writes 'When You are Old'. Meets '90s poets, Johnson and Dowson: Rhymers' Club. Founds London Irish Literary Society. Attempt at realistic novel, *John Sherman*, published. Death of Parnell inspires Yeats.

1892 Produces many love poems. *The Countess Cathleen and Various Legends and Lyrics*. Founds National Literary Society in Dublin. Writes to *The Bookman* on death of Tennyson. Composes 'To Ireland in the Coming Times'.

1893 *The Celtic Twilight* which will give its name to literary era. Three volume *Works of Blake* published. Writes 'The Song of Wandering Aengus'. Poems which will appear as *The Rose* from this period. Second Home Rule Bill defeat.

1894 Meets Mrs Olivia Shakespear with whom he will have first serious affair. Prepares 'Collected' edition of his work. Visits Paris, meets Verlaine. Proposes to Maud Gonne again. First staging of one of his plays: *Land of Heart's Desire*. Visits Lissadell. Meets Lady Gregory, who is inspired by his work on Irish folklore.

1895 *A Book of Irish Verse* and *Poems* published. Yeats visits Oscar Wilde's home to offer support during trial.

1896 Moves to Woburn Buildings. Meets Synge. Political activity. Tours West of Ireland with Symons. Publishes 'The Secret

Rose' and 'He Remembers Forgotten Beauty'. Affair with Olivia Shakespear begins: first sexual experience.

1897 *The Secret Rose* appears: occult stories. Summer spent in Coole Park collaborating with Lady Gregory on folklore and ideas for National Theatre.

1898 Writes 'He Wishes for the Cloths of Heaven'. Travels widely, touring with Maud Gonne. 8th December: she reveals her secret life to him, with devastating emotional consequences. He cannot write poetry for 18 months. Meets James Connolly at his house.

1899 *The Countess Cathleen* performed in Dublin: first season of Irish Literary Theatre. *The Wind Among the Reeds* appears. Visits Maud in France; proposes.

1900 Susan Yeats, his mother, dies. He proposes to Maud Gonne. He takes charge of the new 'Golden Dawn' society.

1901 Yeats proposes again. Experiments with reciting to the psaltery. Yeats meets Hugh Lane, whose offer of paintings for Dublin will cause many problems in years ahead.

1902 *Cathleen ni Houlihan* premiered in Dublin with Maud Gonne in title role. Yeats meets and assists James Joyce. Lily Yeats establishes what will become the Cuala Press: publisher of many of her brother's books.

1903 Maud Gonne marries John MacBride. Irish National Theatre Society formed with Yeats as President. Annie Horniman becomes patron. Yeats tours USA, talks to Roosevelt about fairies, becomes wealthy at last. *In the Seven Woods* published.

1904 Abbey Theatre opens. Lane offers paintings to Dublin.

1905 Yeats receives an edition of Kelmscott Chaucer (designed by William Morris) for his 40th birthday. Hears of breakup of Maud's marriage.

1906 *Poems 1895-1905*. Reads much Elizabethan drama.

1907 Riots at the Abbey performance of Synge's *The Playboy of the Western World*. Yeats denounces audience. Visits Italy.

Affair with Mabel Dickinson. Father emigrates to USA. O'Leary dies. Arthur Symons has breakdown.

1908 *Collected Works* in eight volumes. Stays in Paris with Maud Gonne: probably became lovers this year. Writes 'No Second Troy'. Meets Ezra Pound.

1909 Synge dies after long illness. Yeats edits his work. Money problems.

1910 *The Green Helmet and Other Poems.* Civil List doubles Yeats' income: mocked as 'Pensioner Yeats'. Uncle George Pollexfen dies. Meets Churchill.

1911 Meets future wife Georgie ('George') Hyde-Lees. Home Rule promised for 1912; anti-Home Rule campaign begins.

1912 With Maud Gonne in France. Works with Tagore on Bengali texts. Involved with Society for Psychical Research. Lecture: 'A New Theory of Apparitions'. Writes 'A Coat', defining his new aesthetic.

1913 Works with Ezra Pound at Stone Cottage. 'To a Wealthy Man ...' published as 'The Gift'. Writes 'September 1913'. Ulster Volunteers and Irish Volunteers both founded.

1914 *Responsibilities* published, with epigraph: 'In dreams begins responsibility'. Writes 'The Fisherman'. Begins work on memoirs. US tour; visits France. Pound marries Olivia Shakespear's daughter, Dorothy. Home Rule passed but suspended as First World War begins.

1915 Writes 'Ego Dominus Tuus'. Declines knighthood. Meets T.S. Eliot. Controversy over Metropolitan Art Gallery following Hugh Lane's death on *Lusitania.*

1916 Writes the Noh-influenced drama, *At the Hawk's Well*. The Easter Rising: execution of rebels, including friends of Yeats. He writes 'Easter 1916' and other poems. Proposes to Maud Gonne after John MacBride is executed. Writes 'The Wild Swans at Coole'.

1917 *The Wild Swans at Coole.* Proposes to Iseult Gonne, Maud's daughter. Purchases tower: Thoor Ballylee. Marries George

Hyde-Lees 20th October. Unhappiness until George suddenly starts automatic writing. Florence Farr dies. Sinn Fein successes.

1918 Lady Gregory's son, the airman Robert, killed: Coole destined to be disposed of by his widow. Yeats writes elegies for him. First World War ends. Maud Gonne imprisoned. Writes play, *The Only Jealousy of Emer*. At Oxford, Glendalough, Sligo, Coole: much work with spirits. Writes 'The Phases of the Moon'. Restoring Thoor Ballylee. Lives in Maud's Dublin house, causing ill feeling when she is released.

1919 Daughter, Anne, born: 'A Prayer for My Daughter'. Tempted to tour Japan. Writes 'The Second Coming'. Meeting of Dáil.

1920 USA, Ireland. Begins work on long occult study based on automatic writing: *A Vision*. Constance Markievicz arrested. Black and Tans arrive: atrocities.

1921 Son, Michael, born. *Michael Robartes and the Dancer*. Addresses Oxford Union in memorable seven minute speech on England's treatment of Ireland. Treaty signed ending Anglo-Irish war.

1922 'Senator Yeats' moves to up-market Merrion Square. His father, John, dies. Provisional government takes control. Civil war: in reprisals, 77 executions. Bridge at Thoor Ballylee blown up by Irregulars. *The Trembling of the Veil*. Philip Larkin born.

1923 Nobel Prize for Literature: *The Bounty of Sweden*. De Valera orders ceasefire. Civil war ends. Writes 'Leda and the Swan'.

1924 *The Cat and the Moon and Certain Poems*. Essays.

1925 Controversial Senate speech on divorce. *A Vision* published to general bafflement. *Early Poems and Stories* reprinted. Writes 'The Tower'. Italy.

1926 Commissions designs for new Irish coinage. Visits schools as part of government research: 'Among Schoolchildren'. Writes 'Sailing to Byzantium'. James Merrill born.

1927 Serious lung condition. 'Dialogue of Self and Soul', 'Death'. Kevin O'Higgins assassinated.

1928 *The Tower*, often considered his greatest book. Resigns from Senate, disillusioned after imposition of censorship. Goes to Rapallo. Writes 'Coole Park, 1929'.

1929 Writes 'Mohini Chatterjee'. Final visit to Thoor Ballylee: always keen to hear news of it from pilgrims thereafter. John Montague born.

1930 Writes 'Byzantium'. *Words Upon the Window-pane* produced at the Abbey. Considered as possible Poet Laureate. Ted Hughes born.

1931 Writes 'Coole and Ballylee, 1931'. Begins 'Vacillation'. Oxford degree.

1932 *Words for Music, Perhaps*. Lady Gregory dies (May) after decline. Moves to Riversdale, setting for 'An Acre of Grass'. Forms Irish Academy of Letters. Sylvia Plath born while Yeats on tour of America.

1933 *The Winding Stair and Other Poems. Collected Poems.* Cambridge degree.

1934 Steinach operation causes sexual rejuvenation. Works with Swami on Uphanishads. *Collected Plays*.

1935 *A Full Moon in March*. Meets Auden, who will write his elegy later. 70th birthday banquet. Relationships with actress Margot Ruddock and Marxist writer Ethel Mannin.

1936 Illness. Idiosyncratic *Oxford Book of Modern Verse*. BBC lecture. Writes 'Lapis Lazuli', 'What Then?'.

1937 Revised version of *A Vision*. American poet John Berryman has his own vision of Yeats; eventually meets him at Athenaeum. 'Municipal Gallery Revisited'; begins 'The Circus Animals' Desertion'. Relationship with Edith Shackleton Heald.

1938 *New Poems, The Herne's Egg* (published unperformed). *Purgatory*, his most original play, performed. Olivia Shakespear dies. Vernon Watkins visits and writes 'Yeats in Dublin'. Yeats writes 'Politics', which he always put at the end of his *Collected.* Also completes, 'Long-legged Fly'and 'Under Ben Bulben' in which he gives instructions for his burial in Drumcliff Churchyard.

1939 'Cuchulain Comforted' one of his last poems, his first in *terza rima*. W.B. Yeats dies on 28th January at Roquebrune, France. *Last Poems*. Seamus Heaney born. Michael Longley born. Second World war begins.

1941 Coole Park demolished.

1948 Yeats' body moved to Sligo as requested. His own inscription on stone:

> Cast a cold eye
> On life, on death.
> Horseman, pass by!

1953 Maud Gonne dies.

1

Forced to Choose: Yeats the Man

"He began to talk and so far as I know has continued to do so ever since," said Herbert Grierson after meeting the great Irish poet. Yeats simply loved to talk, whether or not anybody was listening: often it was his way of "thinking aloud and elucidating for himself" as the painter Norah McGuinness discovered when he spoke at her for an entire evening on his new book, *A Vision*, which she had not read. From an early age he would hum and mutter under his breath when composing, too. But as an orator, he had few peers: those who heard him address the Oxford Union in 1921 would not forget it, and his lecture tours of America are littered with accounts of how impressively he could hold an audience's attention. But it was usually the poet's romantic appearance that struck them, the good looks and self-consciously poetic image that Arthur Symons had helped him foster: black jacket, floppy tie, dangling forelock, cigarette at his "translucent lips that were soft and red like the berry of the yew" (Gogarty) – and the famous pince-nez. His sight was bad; he was virtually blind on one side and he had continual eye trouble. In fact, his biography includes many spells of illness, sometimes psychosomatic, as when he was stricken with a fever as soon as he married Georgie Hyde-Lees. But there was also a 'nervous weakness' inherited from his mother's side (the Pollexfens) where there were several manic depressives.

Not all descriptions of Yeats are flattering. There are distinctly undazzled glimpses such as Arthur Waugh's of 1894 ("a tall, sallow, black-haired youth, with the jaw of a monk and a sort of catch in his voice") and many satirical portraits, most famously George Moore's: "Yeats, who had lately returned to us from the States with a paunch, a huge stride, and an immense fur overcoat, rose to speak". It is true that he was exceedingly vain, agonising over which commissioned portrait to put in his Collected edition – John Singer Sargent? Augustus John? He was a gift for caricaturists, becoming "Pensioner Yeats" when he somewhat hypocritically accepted a Civil List Pension (although he did turn down a knighthood) and was frequently drawn in the chinchilla coat, arms flailing, gazing into the Celtic Twilight.

George Moore goes on to describe how Yeats mocked the middle classes in his speech, "and we asked ourselves why Willie Yeats should feel himself called upon to denounce the class to which he himself belonged essentially: on one side excellent mercantile millers and shipowners, and on the other a portrait painter of rare talent ..." The answer is simple: William Butler Yeats was a snob, who believed in the innate superiority of the aristocracy and would speak quite happily of those he considered "our equals" and those he didn't, skating on very thin ice with his views on eugenics and some of his remarks about Mussolini. He was in his element at Lady Gregory's estate in Coole Park. And, of course, life in a tower suited him well, inadequate though it was to the needs of a wife and children. Even in portraits of the youthful Yeats there is what his biographer Stephen Coote sees as a "volatile superiority". At school, there was something "quietly repellent" about him, according to a contemporary. He busied himself with his study of natural history and collecting beetles. One day, he climbed a tree in the school grounds so that he could look down on his fellows: "If when I grow up I am as clever among grown-up men as I am among these boys, I shall be a famous man." Clever he may have been, but not a success at school. He could never master a foreign language (one wonders what his friend, the polyglot Ezra Pound, made of that fact) and spelling remained a mystery to him throughout his life. He failed in his application for a professorship at Trinity College, Dublin because he could not spell 'professor'. But he had trouble with even more fundamental words such as "feal" and "sleap". Punctuation, too, was not a strong point: "I do not understand stops," he said. "I write my work so completely for the ear that I feel helpless when I have to measure pauses by stops and commas." Mercifully, he had sisters to proof-read for him at the Cuala Press.

Yeats was notoriously absent-minded, once downing an entire packet of opiate cough sweets and sleeping for thirty hours. Another time he was told during a Dublin rainstorm that his raincoat was inside out: he swiftly turned it wet side in. He could eat without noticing his food and, one evening at his club, on seeing "a clean glass & port & no plate before me" had to ask whether he had in fact eaten anything. No one was sure, so he ate a meal anyway. More embarrassingly, there is an anecdote about Yeats holding forth at dinner about the qualities (or lack of them) in Eliot's poetry and turning to his neighbour for an opinion only to see a place card being held up with the name "T.S. Eliot" on it. He had an appalling memory for names (speaking publicly of Mussolini as Missolonghi) and a very inaccurate memory for quotations. "Yeats nearly always misquotes," writes Kathleen Raine, an authority on Blake, "but far from proving that he did not therefore know Blake as well as the quoters of chapter and verse, it proves that he knew him so well that he trusted his memory … Blake did not quote accurately either, and for the same reason. Both poets wrote from the fullness of their thought, and not from books of reference."

For all his cultivated vagueness, W.B. – as he was called by his family – did get things done. For example, the edition of Blake Kathleen Raine is referring to, he worked on with Edwin Ellis for four years, one of several such major projects he undertook when he was relatively inexperienced. He believed in precision and thoroughness, which could become obsession. He told Lady Gregory that he had not left a single poem uncompleted since he was seventeen. He was an inveterate reviser, always searching for clarity. He was a great organiser, too, never put off by defeat (something he inherited from the Pollexfens). His work for the Abbey Theatre impressed those who saw it, although he drove some of the actors to despair in his search for perfection. The world of the theatre suited him: aloof though he could be, he liked company and was a good 'networker'. At a young age, he "belonged both to the withdrawn, esoteric world of Mohini Chatterjee and to the abrasive public domain of the Contemporary Club" (Coote). Subsequently, he formed clubs and societies on both sides of the Irish Sea and joined many more, ranging from the Society for Psychical Research to the Rhymers' Club, those "Companions of the Cheshire Cheese …" He also served on a variety of committees when he was a Senator.

Even at the height of his fame, he remained very careful with money, only too aware of his improvident father's difficulties. When funds ran short, he would organise a lecture tour of America (assisted by the invaluable John Quinn). On hearing that he had been awarded the Nobel Prize, his instinctive response was to ask the journalist who told him: "How much, Smyllie, how much is it?" – and then went out to buy a new stair carpet. He would talk about his most mystical publications in terms of what they cost. "It's horribly expensive, £3.3.0 ..." he wrote of *A Vision*. When he found himself responsible for commissioning the new coinage for the Free State, he was in his element, although there were the inevitable quips about adding "ha'pence to the pence".

The interest in magic began early and he told John O'Leary it was "the centre of all that I do". He was convinced that fairies existed because he had seen and heard them in the presence of witnesses in the 1890s; the same was true of spirits. It was as natural for his sister Lily to note that George Pollexfen's death was "heralded by a banshee shriek outside the window" as it was for Yeats and his wife to hear the choir singing at the funeral of Kevin O'Higgins the night before he was assassinated. He attracted the uncanny, as when his Oxford home filled with the smell of Indian incense just as the topic of India was being discussed. He fearlessly informed Bertrand Russell that he could conjure the perfume of roses by simply rubbing his hands. He was always ready to test these experiences, if not with quite the rigour demanded by the Society for Psychical Research, yet he came up with a detailed 'ghost theory'. He himself acknowledged that only one in a thousand mediums communicates anything other than "subconscious experience". Like a much later admirer, Ted Hughes, Yeats would consult astrological charts to guide him at key moments in his life – such as marriage proposals to Maud Gonne and the birth of his children or the direction his writing should take. But the passion for spiritualism which fed his poetry also helped contribute to his reputation for silliness. Seamus Heaney has commented on "the Yeats whom Maud Gonne called 'Silly Willie' and whom W.H. Auden also called 'silly' in his 1939 elegy". But Heaney (who has had his fair share of hostile press attention) admires and understands Yeats' courage, his "protectiveness of his imaginative springs".

There is no doubt about Yeats' eccentricities, from the way he would hurl himself along the pavement to the way he would toss old tea-leaves out of his window in Merrion Square. There are stories about him becoming glued to fly-paper, of swallowing his hair with his spaghetti – but carrying on talking, talking ... The loquaciousness was not something he could help, and at the height of his fame influential fans would try and worm their way into his company just to be lectured, but there was certainly an element of 'pose', or of 'mask' in everything he did. Who else but W.B. Yeats would have toured the country reciting his works to the accompaniment of the psaltery? Whether he laughed at his own follies is not clear, although there is increasing self-mockery in his later poetry and in the 1880s he had been prepared to poke fun at the serious business of Theosophy: "A sad accident happened at Madame Blavatsky's lately, I hear. A big materialist sat on the astral double of a poor young Indian. It was sitting on the sofa and he was too material to be able to see it. Certainly a sad accident." There are not many such examples of the light-hearted Yeats in his published work.

The serious business of Yeats' life was friendship and love. Women were drawn to him and felt protective of him. Many were considerably older, which may tell us something about the void he felt as his mother drifted into her own world. After a late start he had a string of lovers, although Brenda Maddox suggests that only Olivia Shakespear and Mabel Dickinson were 'satisfactory' from the sexual point of view. Others stood on the sidelines and worshipped or – like Marianne Moore in one of her letters – noted "the hands of a hereditary royalist who never picked up a stone or touched his own shoes". Maud Gonne was more muse than lover; Lady Gregory was a friend in art. One of Yeats' most quoted lines is "And say my glory was I had such friends", written after revisiting the Municipal Gallery – which institution, of course, also made him quite a few enemies. Leaving the pantheon of enemies aside, Yeats' friendships must be acknowledged. The creative ones are of particular interest: George Russell (AE), sharing his fascination with things mystical; J.M. Synge, mythologised in so many of W.B.'s poems; Arthur Symons, "the only man I think with whom I have had an entirely intimate and understanding friendship"; Ezra Pound, who in a concentrated period at Stone Cottage in Sussex in 1913 affected Yeats' verse as dramatically as he would Eliot's;

James Joyce, who told him he was "too old" to be of use to him, yet whose *Ulysses* was highly respected by 'Pensioner Yeats'... He was generous, too, to young writers or those whose names were not so well known: to L.A.G. Strong, for example, when he was at Oxford ("from being tongue-tied and reverent, I was drawn into a confidence ... which helped slowly to build me into something approaching an adult") and to the Welsh poet Vernon Watkins, whose visit in 1938 had a profound impact. Watkins' long poem, 'Yeats in Dublin' evokes the occasion in an appropriately Yeatsian style:

> With visionary footsteps
> Slow, he crossed the room,
> He who had made the dead lips sing
> And celebrate love in doom,
> About him the sages
> Of Byzantium.

As to his family, it is generally felt that Yeats was rather a distant father and certainly that is the view Anne and Michael expressed in a television documentary: he was an old man and a busy man when they were born. Yet Anne remembers he was "a mean croquet player" (and didn't like parsnips); while Michael recalled him telling amusing stories "for the children". As a son, Yeats was perhaps less than attentive to his father whom he nevertheless admired hugely, and whose boldness of spirit liberated the poet's genius. And towards his sisters he could be something of a bully. His young brother, the painter Jack Yeats he kept at a distance, unwilling to pass comment or become involved in his increasingly successful career. There were certain political tensions between them, too. Yeats liked to be his own man, but he was never one to shun controversy, unafraid to stand and denounce a rioting audience at The Abbey Theatre or to tell the Dáil what he thought about their divorce law or to lecture America on their need for an aristocracy. He had a fiery temper and like those leaders he admired – disgraced Parnell, assassinated O'Higgins – he was prepared to be unpopular.

He was also shamelessly candid: his frank memoirs about youthful experiences when he was 15 and alone on the sands on the Third Rosses "tortured by sexual desire" caused much mirth and the odd witty squib (see the limerick on p19). Oscar Wilde, whom he met in the 1880s, would surely have approved of such openness, but might not have understood why Yeats is celebrated above all for having developed and gone on developing. After all, Wilde said "only mediocrities develop". Yet this is what T.S. Eliot especially admired in him and what Seamus Heaney chose to highlight when he wrote *Yeats as an Example?* He quotes lines from 'The Choice', written in 1931, and originally planned as part of a final stanza for 'Coole and Ballylee, 1931'. Many artists must have remembered these words in times of crisis, when 'perfection' seemed impossible and too many sacrifices were having to be made. They are lines that barely seem adequate to the richness of both Yeats' life and his work, but they remind us (as Heaney says) of "the way the courage of his vision did not confine itself to rhetorics but issued in actions":

> The intellect of man is forced to choose
> Perfection of the life or of the work,
> And if it take the second must refuse
> A heavenly mansion, raging in the dark.

2

Public Dreams, Private Myths: the Mythographer

"A myth is a public dream, a dream is a private myth," wrote Joseph Campbell. W.B.Yeats knew the value of both, drawing on myth and dream from his earliest creative years (his mid-teens) to the very end of his life in the 1930s, when all about him were turning to "the factory, the metropolis", to "the man who travels to his work by Tube". The tension in his poetry between the inner and the outer world, between the experienced and the imagined, is probably a result of childhood experience, much of which he would recall as painful. The distinguished American critic, Randall Jarrell, noted shortly after Yeats' death how the poet was caught between:

> the real and detestable world of London, where he was imprisoned and miserable; and ... the ideal world of Sligo, that he longed for all year, revisited every summer. One was the world of trade and industry and science, of smoke and streets and school, of the coarse dull English; the other world was all that he loved and remembered, the world of myth and superstition and romance, his own country.
>
> (*The Development of Yeats's Sense of Reality,* 1942)

Yeats' public dream begins with the poems of the so-called 'Celtic Twilight' to be found in the opening two sections of his *Collected Poems*, where what he later called an essentially religious instinct "made a new religion, almost an infallible church of poetic tradition, of a fardel of stories, and of personages, and of emotions". With the glamorous example of his eccentric Sligo uncle, George Pollexfen, the intellectual ambitions of his father, and later the guidance of the nationalist, John O'Leary (together with the adoring interest of young ladies like Katharine Tynan) the youthful Yeats soon found what mattered to him most in life: not nature – for all his beetle collecting – but 'supernature', whether fairy, goddess, spirit or legendary hero. His father would exasperatedly try and persuade him to write more about real life, but the poet wanted to follow mystical paths – and, after all, John B.Yeats himself had recited all kinds of fantastical verse to his son when he was younger. The teenage Willie read all the Romantic literature he could find, including Standish O'Grady's retelling of Irish legends. He soon began collecting folk-tales and fairy stories himself, writing plays (and even a novel, to appease J.B.); but it was as a poet that he knew he would make a name. Thinking perhaps of the boy's distant, sickly mother, but knowing also of his difficulties with women, J.B. Yeats suggested in his unpublished memoirs "that the foundation of the artistic nature is affectionateness which, denied its satisfaction, as it always is, in real life, turns to the invention of art and poetry."

Some of Yeats' early poems are lengthy, notably 'The Wanderings of Oisin' (pronounced *Usheen*), which he began working on in 1887 and was to be the title poem of his first collection, later reorganised into *Crossways* for his *Collected* . But for today's readers it is likely to be the shorter poems that appeal. The style is Pre-Raphaelite, mannered, full of folksy gestures, self-consciously artificial from the opening inversions of the first poem, 'The Song of the Happy Shepherd' ("The woods of Arcady are dead,/And over is their antique joy;/Of old the world on dreaming fed;/Grey Truth is now her painted toy"). The use of the shepherd as a mouthpiece is a well-established pastoral convention, as is the classical context. 'Truth' will, of course, come to seem less 'grey' to Yeats as his career develops and he will eventually find himself rhyming it elegiacally with 'youth'. He is interested now in being true to the myths that move him, rather than to the language in which he describes them. It will not be until *Responsibilities*, fifteen years later, that he will realise that he is making "a coat/Covered with embroideries" and that "there's more enterprise/In walking naked". Yet, as C.H. Sisson has pointed out, these early lyrics are keys with which to unlock the essential later poems.

It has to be appreciated just how serious Yeats was about his explorations of myth and fairytale. He believed in the existence of fairies and was not afraid to argue the point with the most hard-headed rationalists of his day, although he had a sense of humour on the subject, too. As so many Irish folk-tales involve fairies, and visits to an occluded other world, it is a natural progression from the mythology of these early poems to the spiritualism of his later collections. *Crossways* includes, too, his first forays into Theosophy and eastern mysticism, under the influence of Mohini Chatterjee, but it is myth rather than magic that fascinates him as yet. The best poems are those that tell a story rather than wallowing in description. 'The Madness of King Goll' is effective in this way, introducing for the first time a characteristic Yeatsian device: the refrain. We also meet the word "tumult", which will thunder through the *Collected Works.* It is remarkable how many favourite Yeats words turn up even in this early work: Randall Jarrell lists them: "*dream, rose, heart, lonely, wandering, gentle, sorrow, sweet, mournful, holy, tender, quiet, faery, Druid, beauty, peace, lofty, high, pitiful, wan, murmur, worn, grief, tears, weary, sigh, old, desolate, piteous, faint, dreaming, foam, flame, fade, woven, tremble, shadowy, grey, dim, white, pale*" and goes on to contrast them with a list from the later poems: *foul, passionate, ignorant, malicious, abstract, crazy, lunatic, mad, bitter,* etc. Yet, however contrived and fanciful the language of *Crossways* and *The Rose*, we always feel that there is a flesh and blood man talking to us: there is a distinctive Yeatsian voice, an inescapable Yeatsian music, which mesmerises and makes one suspend criticism. As William H. Pritchard puts it in his *Lives of the Modern Poets*, one of the most trenchant accounts of Yeats' achievement, we end up "believing something we know not quite what, except that it sounds marvellous".

The music in the language has made Yeats' early poems particularly popular with song-writers and *Crossways* includes the love lyric 'Down by the Salley Gardens', known in versions by Benjamin Britten and others. 'The Stolen Child' was very effectively set by the band 'The Waterboys' in the 1990s for a CD celebrating Yeats' work (*Now and in Time to Be*). The verses were recited grittily, the chorus sung, with a haunting drone accompaniment. This fine poem uses the belief, familiar from *A Midsummer Night's Dream*, that fairies like to kidnap boys and girls, sometimes substituting a changeling (which is why lines from it are quoted in Spielberg's film *A.I.*) Yeats' scene-setting is restrained and colourful, without too much of the theatre back-drop about it. The music of the verse distracts us from any charges of silliness. It could be a poem for children, but it has an adult darkness concealed in it. And there is a concreteness of observation beyond the "dim grey sands" and "ferns that drop their tears", when the poet writes how "brown mice bob/ Round and round the oatmeal-chest". "Bob" is precisely what mice do when you are trying to trap them, although Yeats probably did not care, any more than he did when it was pointed out to him concerning a line from another early poem, "the peahens dance on a smooth lawn", that peahens don't in fact dance. His wonderful response was: "With the poultry yards I have no concern". Yeats wrote to Katharine Tynan in March 1888 that he had noticed, in preparing his poetry for his first book, "that it is almost all a flight into fairyland from the real world, and a summons to that flight. The Chorus to 'The Stolen Child' sums it up – that it is not the poetry of insight and knowledge, but of longing and complaint – the cry of the heart against necessity."

The specifically Irish mythology takes an even stronger hold in *The Rose*, and we sense his dreaminess condensing into symbolism. The opening poem, 'To the Rose Upon the Rood of Time', is usually printed in italics, the typographical equivalent of a black velvet jacket and *pince-nez*. And there is no point in asking ourselves what the effect would be if Fergus were not such a magical name. Yeats adored reeling off grand names in verse as much as he liked dropping them into his conversation: he was quick to compliment those who were able to declaim such quasi-Homeric lists with authority. Roy Foster tells how the poet praised one of the actors at the Abbey Theatre for "the emotional intensity with which he declaimed the names of old Irish heroes", to which the actor replied: "Sure I thought they were mountains." Gods are not called Paddy or Willie any more than they are called Ben Bulben; and Yeats had already proved by the last decade of the nineteenth century that he could write about Moll Magee and Huntsman Rody. 'To the Rose Upon the Rood of Time' is his "tragic buskin", embroidered in compound adjectives, soulful repetitions, meaningful proper nouns and much use of "bitter" and "ancient". As he would write in his great final poem, "Players and painted stage took all my love/And not those things that they were emblems of."

The players in this pageant of 1893 are Fergus, Emer (pronounced *Aymir* or *Ayvir*) and particularly Cuchulain (*Koo-hullin*). 'Cuchulain's Fight with the Sea' is one of the longer pieces, composed (with much revision) in Yeats' beloved rhyming couplets: it tells its story with dramatic authority, for all the archaic diction and the echoes of Matthew Arnold's 'Sohrab and Rustum'. In making Cuchulain an emblem of an independent Ireland, already we feel the poet looking for something less parochial than 'mere' fairy tales, while finding a way of writing about his own battle with uncontainable forces that were expressing themselves in some of the book's love poems. Already, his 'private myths' are driving the poetry, Cuchulain becoming "a heroic figure because he was creative joy separated from fear", as Yeats put it. He would revisit this archetype in 'The Circus Animals' Desertion' (1938); and in the fortnight before his death, turning for the only time in his life to Dante's *terza rima*, he would write 'Cuchulain Comforted'. Seamus Heaney has singled out this poem for its "strange ritual of surrender, a rite of passage from life into death, but a rite whose meaning is subsumed into song, the otherness of art".

The sequence of 'Rose' poems, with its idealisation of the feminine archetype to complement the masculinity of Cuchulain, is unlikely to delay readers as they hurry on to familiar friends such as 'The Lake Isle of Innisfree' , 'The Pity of Love' and 'When You are Old'. Nevertheless, we see Yeats working out themes that will sustain many later, greater poems. 'What does the 'Rose' mean?' is a question the new reader is likely to ask and it is a question that time does not take away. Yes, it is Ireland, it is the 'eternal feminine', it is Maud Gonne, it is 'beauty and wisdom', it is suffering, it is the beginnings of a Rosicrucian philosophy ('rood' = cross), it is Blake's 'Song of Experience' and much more besides. Enough, indeed, to fill several shelves of academic studies, as any student of Yeats soon finds out. It is, as a poem in his next collection suggests, a 'Secret Rose', and that perhaps is how he wishes it to remain. For those who desire to tease out all the possibilities, that rich and enigmatic poem from *The Wind Among the Reeds* is a good one to ponder: there is tumult (not to say tumescence) aplenty, together with Magi, Druids, Fand, Emer, "wine-stained wanderers in deep woods" and some of the most memorably baffling apocalyptic lines he ever wrote.

The important thing for readers is not to be put off at an early stage by this kind of puzzle: Yeats' meanings are in many ways simpler than we expect, his work from the 1890s (to quote a later Irish poet and biographer of Yeats,) "suddener than we fancy it." These are, I think, poems to be heard and loved rather than deciphered: there is plenty of much more worthwhile deciphering to come.

The Rose offers us more fairyland – or "faeryland" as Yeats rather pointlessly insists, incapable as he was of even spelling 'feeling' (*fealing*) – more dreaming, much imagery of idyllic fantasy places such as Innisfree, but the love poems are beginning to dominate. Yeats had not yet had a sexual encounter, but the reality of love is beginning to intrude through the mythology like a new volcanic island boiling out of the sea. Some of the most moving poems are those in which love and myth merge. So, in 'The White Birds' the birds of fairyland, which are "said to be white as snow" and imagery of the Danaan (*De-nâyan*) Islands (a region of fairyland) mask an anapaestic outpouring of longing for Maud Gonne, who had just refused him. And Fergus is the looked-for but vanished hero, the consolatory figure to the lovelorn Willie brooding 'Upon love's bitter mystery', as O'Leary or Connolly will be later. Yet it is the word-music that hypnotises in 'Who Goes with Fergus' (Eliot thought it "perfect"), the lyric mastery, so easy to parody, but impossible to carry off without Yeats' conviction, as the hordes of forgotten 1890s poets testify. Who goes with AE now? Or Lionel Johnson, the book's dedicatee?

The Rose ends with a defiant new note. 'To Ireland in the Coming Times' (another of those italicized poems) declares that here is a poet conscious of his role as spokesman for a new Ireland that will be born of the old. Speaking in octosyllabic couplets associated more with Swift than the Romantics, he has walked downstage from the mystical backdrop to remind his audience almost apologetically ("Nor may I less be counted one/With Davis, Mangan, Ferguson ...") that he is conscious of his responsibilities to the canon of Irish literature, but that he cannot help acting out this fairy drama for them. That the rose symbolism is something from which he must move on is suggested by "the red-rose-bordered hem". It is now on the fringes of experience, an image in a passing procession: he is free to move away and beyond it.

Nevertheless, he is still being summoned by supernatural forces, as shown by the opening poem of his next collection, 'The Hosting of the Sidhe' (a name for the ancient gods or the 'faery folk', pronounced, perhaps with psychological significance, *She*): "Away, come away:/Empty your heart of its mortal dream" is their rallying cry, a fanfare that opens *The Wind Among the Reeds* (1899). The ballad, 'The Host of the Air' is less a piece of atmospherics, much more complete as a poem. It tells, with a nod towards Keats' pale knight-at-arms, the story of O'Driscoll, who "drove with a song/The wild duck and the drake/From the tall and the tufted reeds/Of the drear Hart Lake", and dreamed of his fiancée, only to see her carried off by "the host of the air". The ballad metre always brings out the best in Yeats: it enables him to move things forward, yet to dwell just long enough on telling descriptive details, highlighting with repetition and echo. The metre is so insistent that he is able to risk obscurity and melodrama without the reader noticing, much as we do not quarrel with the words of a pop-song if the tune is good. All those ballads his father, his nurse and various neighbours read to him as a boy ensured he had a good ear for this particular form: the subtle use of alliteration to energise key lines ("Until one bore Bridget his bride") and the circularity of the structure: "O'Driscoll drove with a song", "O'Driscoll scattered the cards/And out of his dream awoke", coming back finally to lines we heard earlier, in the same way that he "... heard high up in the air/A piper piping away,/And never was piping so sad,/And never was piping so gay."

The word "gay" is one we have to accustom ourselves to in Yeats: it is crucial to his philosophy and he likes to use it as a rhyme word, as a culmination: "Their ancient, glittering eyes, are gay"('Lapis Lazuli'). It would be fascinating to know how the older poet, always eager to refine and update his diction, would have reacted to the development in its meaning in the late twentieth century.

The Wind Among the Reeds includes several richly orchestrated, rather overblown, show-pieces like 'The Unappeasable Host' ("Desolate winds that cry over the wandering sea;/Desolate winds that hover in the flaming West ...") which it is hardly surprising to hear were much loved by the composer Arnold Bax, who even wrote a tone poem using Yeats' title, 'Into the Twilight'. Set amongst such pieces are simple tales or brilliant song-like lyrics such as 'The Song of Wandering Aengus'. We do not need to know who Aengus was or that the poem is in fact an *aisling* ('ash-ling'), a traditional Irish genre in which the poet encounters a supernatural female. It is a wonderfully memorable poem, the quintessence of early Yeats: not stretching beyond what he can at this stage manage, but handling to perfection the skills he has acquired, without giving way to his obsessions. This is the kind of writing that even the arch-critic Ezra Pound could admire: the way he avoids abstraction, proving that this was not just something he suddenly learnt after the Easter Rising. Indeed, he lost the facility for writing lyrics that sound so spontaneous. More than one critic has commented on this, finding them (to quote C.H. Sisson on *Words for Music, Perhaps*) "too preconceived to impress us as poetry".

The love poems well up and take control of *The Wind Among the Reeds*, and these will be discussed in the next chapter, but the symbolism, the metaphors, the 'masks' Yeats uses are drawn again and again from Irish mythology. We feel by the time we reach 'The Secret Rose' that there is more going on in Yeats' imagination than he can cope with: he has to move on. To understand Yeats' greatness, this determination to develop has to be understood. Having mentioned Bax earlier, perhaps we should look at a better parallel in Bax's friend Jean Sibelius, who was born in the same year as the poet. Had Sibelius written all his symphonies in the style of his first two he would have been a phenomenon like Bax, (who did just that in his seven, which are almost indistinguishable). But Sibelius took a new direction with each symphony thereafter, solving a different problem in each case. This is what makes Sibelius one of the most important composers of the twentieth century; and it is what makes Yeats perhaps the most important poet. As T.S. Eliot, his chief rival to that title, explained in the first annual Yeats Lecture, he managed to maintain the "integrity of his passion for his art and his craft" and to "remain always a contemporary".

Although *In the Seven Woods* (1904) and *The Green Helmet and Other Poems* (1910) are very much transitional books, we see the spirit of Yeats' imagination at work, shaping new forms, new ways of saying what he has to say (not least in the remarkable 'Adam's Curse', which will be discussed elsewhere). Influenced perhaps by his editing of Blake's poetry, Yeats begins to adopt personae from mythology or from his esoteric studies—Red Hanrahan puts in his first appearance, later to be joined by Owen Aherne, Michael Robartes. These figures will become increasingly important mouthpieces for him. When Yeats uses conventional mythologies in these poems of his middle period, it is more often than not to show how he is disillusioned, so in 'Under the Moon' he mournfully lists all the heroes who bring him no joy. There is further recourse to Homeric material, most famously in 'No Second Troy', but we have moved away from the stagey world of the first books. Indeed, Yeats has experienced and writes about the real stage now (brilliantly buzzing *plays/ways/day's/knave/business* like a gadfly):

> ... My curse on plays
> That have to be set up in fifty ways,
> On the day's war with every knave and dolt,
> Theatre business, management of men.

But he can only clinch his frustration by returning to his mythical sources, to the idea of a Pegasus, a god-driven holy colt that is battering at his heart to be set free:

> I swear before the dawn comes round again
> I'll find the stable and pull out the bolt.

The aesthetic confusion is concisely expressed in the penultimate poem from the 1910 book, 'All Things Can Tempt Me', where for all the directness of the opening lines, the poet seems not quite certain that keeping "a sword upstairs" is modern enough (he will have no doubts later, with Sato's blade and a winding staircase), and only knows how to use plain talk about keeping silent.

Responsibilities (1914) is traditionally taken as the turning point in Yeats' poetic career, with its epigraph "In dreams begins responsibility" and the poet's renewed concern for the flesh and blood of his own ancestry ("Pardon, old fathers ..."), his literary peers ('Companions of the Cheshire Cheese ...'), and contemporary Irish politics; but it is still to a myth of Ireland that he turns in the long opening poem ('The Grey Rock'). Only in the very last poem ('A Coat') does he make his aesthetic case for abandoning "old mythologies" – not all mythologies, only old ones. *The Wild Swans at Coole*, his 1919 collection, is haunted by myth: the swans cannot but conjure a whole range of stories, which Yeats now chooses not to tell, emphasising instead the simple fact that they mate for life. The mute swans are allowed to sing in our imaginations, as Tuonela does behind Sibelius' cor anglais. The mythology that is absorbing Yeats by the end of this collection is something quite new and extraordinary, born of his wife's automatic writing and his "system" (*A Vision,* 1925). These occult territories will come to dominate some of his greatest late poems and will be discussed in another chapter, but they are in a neighbouring province to 'Faeryland', their inhabitants having much in common with Yeats' early gods and goddesses. 'The Phases of the Moon', like 'The Secret Rose', is a poem that shows Yeats struggling to find a new understanding and losing clarity in the verse. He does best when he is almost offhand, as in 'The Cat and the Moon', where we do not need to know what the moon signifies to divine the poem's meaning. Yet Yeats is always capable of defying common sense and producing a poem which is utterly elusive and at the same time utterly compelling. In the case of 'The Second Coming', from *Michael Robartes and the Dancer* (1921), he produced a poem fragments of which have dropped into everyday usage in defiance of its obscurities. Many a journalist has reached for the phrase "things fall apart" or "the centre cannot hold" or even "the ceremony of innocence is drowned" to express something of the mood of our age. Yet it might have been thought that 'Easter 1916' had the topical edge in that collection.

Subsequent collections (*The Tower*, 1928; *The Winding Stair and Other Poems*, 1933; *Parnell's Funeral and Other Poems*, 1935, *New Poems*, 1938 and *Last Poems*, 1939) see Yeats conjuring with the imagery of Byzantium, evoking a mythical land of golden artifice not so far from the faery hills, and touching on elements of Chinese and Japanese culture. Nor has he abandoned earlier concerns: he looks to Greece again for his masterpiece, 'Leda and the Swan', but most strikingly he is forging myths from the stuff of his own autobiography, determined "to make all out of myself" even if he is "a tattered coat upon a stick". Perhaps he remembered some words of Oscar Wilde, whom he met in the 1880s: "I think a man should invent his own myth." As C.H. Sisson points out:

> reading 'The Tower' we learn nothing of the old man, who took to reading detective stories and, if he ignored the death of his friends, did so not because he had a full-fashioned soul but out of selfishness, like the rest of us, and particularly the old.

On the other hand, we hear much of the tower he inhabits, the sword he owns, symbolic bees, emblematic swans, significant ancestors, archetypal visitors; he is not averse to mythologising living friends along with himself if it serves his purpose.

Philip Larkin, who was lastingly influenced by Yeats, but could not find a place for him in the world he inhabited, used to talk dismissively of a "myth-kitty". When the author of 'Church Going' donated "an Irish sixpence" in that country church (the excuse being that he was in Ireland at the time) he was perhaps unconsciously making an offering to his former idol. He must have envied Yeats the resources he could draw on: he, too, would use the stuff of his own life ("stuff your pension …") but it would never rival the richness that Yeats found in his own "rag and bone shop" and all he could use to orchestrate his lyrics was nihilistic vagueness, as at the end of 'High Windows' or at best the arrow-shower in 'The Whitsun Weddings'. Mythology was the very life-blood of Yeats' work. He saw everything (through his semi-blindness) in terms of myth. Fairies were real, spirits were real; his friends and lovers perhaps less so, certainly no more. Even Maud Gonne was loved as much for the spiritualist quest they conducted as for herself and her politics. Reading Yeats' poems, then, one has to bear in mind that he saw the world symbolically, that this life on earth was for him one scene in a much greater theatrical production, that most events were to him like the masque in *The Tempest*, ("We are such stuff /As dreams are made on"), with just the occasional incident striking him as 'real' ("I had forgot that foul conspiracy …"). Only Prospero could see the bigger picture.

3

Love Poet, Lyric Poet

It is for his love poetry that Yeats is most widely read, although in life he was an untypical lover, not enjoying intercourse until he was in his thirties and then with a married woman, Olivia Shakespear. Generally he seemed to find greater ease in solitary pleasures, something he confessed to in his memoirs and found hurled back at him by a wag when it became known that the Abbey Theatre's patron, the tea heiress Annie Horniman, had a serious crush on him:

> What a pity that Miss Annie Horniman
> When she wants to seduce or suborn a man
> Should choose Willie Yeats
> Who still masturbates
> And at any rate isn't a horny man.

Frustrations apart, there had been strong teenage feelings for his cousin, Laura Armstrong, then a passionate literary correspondence with Katharine Tynan, and a slow-burning fuse of an affair with actress Florence Farr. There were possibilities with the artist Althea Gyles and the Gore-Booth sisters ("both beautiful, one a gazelle"), and the more tangible offerings of "medical gymnast and masseuse" Mabel Dickinson and fellow spiritualist Alick Schepeler. Although he ended up marrying someone half his age (George Hyde-Lees "smoked and drank", Brenda Maddox reminds us. "Her conversation was peppered with the *Christs, hells* and *damns* of the liberated woman") many of those closest to him were older, and of course the most intimate and creatively vital of these was Lady Gregory.

By the latter end of his life, there were adoring women on all sides, as Brenda Maddox's book, *George's Ghosts*, makes clear. But the gold thread running through any biography of W.B. Yeats is inevitably Maud Gonne – with perhaps a silver thread for her daughter Iseult, to whom Yeats also proposed. The obsession can be dated from 30th January 1889, when "a hansom drew up to our door at Bedford Park … and the troubling of my life began." Long before the relationship was eventually consummated (most probably 1908-9), Maud became the poet's muse. She was, says his daughter Anne, "disastrously beautiful". Perhaps not conventionally so, judging from photographs, but there was something of the goddess in her bearing (she was six feet tall), her "apple-blossom" complexion, her bronze hair and eyes. He first asked her to marry him in 1891, but she was always very clear that Yeats simply would not do as a husband – quite apart from the fact that she already had a secret family in France. Roy Foster points out the revealing fact that for at least six years after this, she would continue to begin her letters formally: "My dear Mr Yeats". The story of Maud Gonne's unhappy, unsettled life is too involved to tell here, suffice to say that she was extremely wealthy and committed to fight the cause of Irish independence, and that she lost her son to meningitis very early on in her relationship with Willie. This event almost destroyed her and left her poet friend feeling quite inadequate. Yeats pithily (if somewhat inaccurately) summed up the relationship: "She was complete; I was not." It is worth remembering the question Louis MacNeice so shrewdly asked: "If Maud Gonne had married Yeats, what would have happened to his poetry?"

A glance through the history of English (if not Irish) poetry shows that until the twentieth century the love poem holds sway and the love poem is frequently a lyric, a short, intense expression of feeling. Thus, we can trace back through Dowson, via Robert and Elizabeth Barrett Browning to Landor's 'Ianthe', roving Byron, Shelley's 'Jane', Wordsworth's 'Lucy', skipping past Swift's rather unlyrical 'Stella' to Lovelace's 'Alcea' and Donne's innumerable lyrical conquests, and suddenly we are in a landscape made up entirely of love sonnets. Curiously, Yeats was not a great sonneteer except for the one masterpiece, 'Leda and the Swan', which we shall discuss shortly. He knew better than to emulate so many Elizabethans addressing their mistresses, although he paid homage to the convention in 'When You are Old'. And perhaps the sonnet is not truly a lyric: there has to be an argument of some kind going on in it.

Yeats liked to quarrel, with others or with himself, but could not really argue. In debate with friends he would silence proceedings with a remark such as "Ah, but that was before the peacock cried!" Yet in perservering with the lyric and the love poem in the face of Modernism and the 1930s poets, he was putting a case for continuity. He had learnt that good poets do not have to go around on stilts, but nothing could change the fact that there were still only two worthwhile themes for a poet: death and love.

Since W.B. Yeats' work develops so uniquely, it is dangerous to generalise too much, but it is true to say that he produced love poems and lyric poems at all stages of his career. The lovers in the earlier ones tend to sound more conventional, conceived in the embrace of literature. 'Down by the Salley Gardens', for example, from September 1888, has the flavour of Ferguson's old Irish poems. In Yeats' lyric the suggestion is that the speaker had a chance to make love to the girl under the canopy of 'salleys' or willows ("She bid me take love easy ...") but he turned her down, perhaps out of "young and foolish" puritan scruples. It could be read the other way round, but the "tears" sound more like those of a boy who has missed his chance.

The love poems in *The Rose* generally rely on what F.R. Leavis called "a certain esoteric languor", yet 'The Pity of Love' and (particularly) 'When You are Old' (1891) succeed because of their lyrical tautness. Composed just at the time when Maud Gonne was in agonies of grief over the death of her son (her adopted son, Yeats believed), 'When You are Old' confronts the insecurity the poet feels knowing that his beloved is so generally admired. He is different, he tells her: he (as his poems have) would have stayed with her into her old age – something we might take with a pinch of salt knowing Yeats' taste for youth and beauty. But he has been driven with 'Love' to hide in ethereal realms. The poem uses iambic pentameter in three quatrains, rhymed *abba*. The first line could not be plainer – here is Yeats typically brooding on old age when he is not yet thirty – and glides close to sentimentality, but avoids it with the kind of sharpness one admires in Browning's 'Meeting at Night', though without that poem's sexual undertow. The economy is admirable: she, not just her hair, will be grey; "full of sleep" suggests ripeness for death; and despite inversions of the kind Pound would want to excise ("of their shadows deep") the momentum is sustained by making each stanza an entire clause. The lyric consists of three scenes, beginning where a Shakespearean sonnet would end ("and this gives life to thee") as an old woman takes down a book to remind herself of the poet's words. The central scene is a brief pageant of jealousy and devotion: the word love appears for the first time, repeated in each of the four lines. The "pilgrim soul" is a perfectly placed enigma, such as all successful lyrics need, but suggesting Shakespeare again – the lovers' sonnet within *Romeo and Juliet* ("Good pilgrim, you do wrong …"). After all this, it somehow seems appropriate that it was a woman called Shakespear who gave Yeats his first sexual experience. The poem's third scene makes the "fire" of the opening a symbol of love, and contrasts the potential behind those imprisoning "bars" with the cold distant fires of the stars they rhyme with. "Murmur" marks the first metrical shift from the iambic, preparing us for the transformation of love from something felt and quietly shared to an inaccessible personification, a vanished god. The picture blends in the imagination with one of sparks disappearing up the chimney.

Of the various love lyrics in *The Rose*, few manage quite the intensity of longing that Yeats expresses not for any woman but for that childhood island, Innisfree. He was more in love with dreams than anything else, but it is curious how the lyric (which he came to hate) was inspired by staring from "the pavements grey" at a ball on a jet of water in a London shop. The bell-beat of those three stressed monosyllables, "deep heart's core", is hard to better, and hard to read without hearing Yeats' own incantatory performance – one of the few poems he did put on record. Douglas Goldring tells of an occasion when the tone-deaf poet was invited to 'sing' his poem, the result being stifled giggles until "I received the impact of one of the poet's many glances from behind his pince-nez." 'The Lake Isle of Innisfree' (1888) was originally much looser: Yeats was an inveterate reviser, frequently writing his poems out in prose first.

The abundance of love poetry in *The Wind Among the Reeds* displays a "fresh unliterary spontaneity" (Leavis); nevertheless, the same formulae are being applied, for example the poet's conviction that life is somehow conspiring to pollute the purity of his love. In 'The Pity of Love' in the previous book, he listed all the things that "threaten the head that I love"; here, he does much the same in 'The

Lover Tells of the Rose in his Heart': "All things uncomely and broken, all things worn out and old .../Are wronging your image ..." But Yeats is always moving forward, trying something new. So, he gives us the 'Old Mother's' view of young love in ten rasping lines (again, there is a recording of Yeats reading this). She reminds us in an effortful metre that it's all very well talking about the fire of love (as Yeats had in 'When You are Old'), but who has to *make* the fire? Who has to bring up the children? Not that Willie knew a great deal about housekeeping or indeed childcare. There is a well known picture of him looking distinctly ill at ease with Michael and Anne, his book judiciously placed beside him ready (as Brenda Maddox says) "to be picked up as soon as the photographer has finished".

The very formal titles of the love poems in *The Wind Among the Reeds* disguise their autobiographical nature; their original titles were more revealing. Structurally, they tend to be similar, so 'He Remembers Forgotten Beauty', in which the beloved is elevated to an archetype for all beauty (mention of Helen of Troy comes in later poems) moves to a grand, mysterious finale much as 'When You are Old' did. The later poem was originally titled 'Michael Robartes Remembers Forgotten Beauty' and the beauty here is usually taken to be Olivia Shakespear. It should not be assumed that all the love poems are about Maud Gonne. One that certainly must be is 'He Wishes for the Cloths of Heaven' (1898 – originally 'Aedh wishes ...', another of his personae, representing fire burning by itself, the devoted imagination). The biographical context here is interesting, as Willie was at the time hoping for some kind of peace settlement with Maud, but he was also very conscious of his poverty and this deterred him from asking her to marry him (even though she was a millionairess by today's standards). Just as he received the proofs for *The Wind Among the Reeds*, she revealed that she was not in fact keeping herself pure and consecrated to Ireland, but was married to the journalist and politician Lucien Millevoye and had given birth to two of his children. Yeats could hardly bring himself to write poetry for another 18 months.

The syntax of 'He Wishes for the Cloths of Heaven' is again impressive: the way a single sentence (or perhaps two) threads in and out of the metrical fabric, stitching alliterations and heraldic colours as it goes, our expectations of rhyme greeted instead by needlepoint repetitions: *cloths*, *light*, *feet*, *dreams*. Yeats employs a sonnet-like division between the first five lines and the last three. If this could happen ... But it cannot, says "grey truth". Did Yeats hesitate over that "because" in the last line? Perhaps "for"? Perhaps nothing? Or "You are treading on my dreams"?

'The Cap and Bells' (1893) could not be more of a contrast. The ballad form often sharpens the shadows in his work, and the metre forces him to clarity and purposefulness. This is a touching tale of a jester in love, who offers gifts in the colours of his trade to the young queen. She is unmoved by his monkish soul "in a straight blue garment" and shuts the window on it; his heart "in a red and quivering garment" sings to her unsuccessfully. "'I have cap and bells,' he pondered, 'I will send them to her and die'". She takes these, lets his motley heart and soul back in, and she is happy: but the jester is dead. It is a brilliant, unpretentious piece of balladry, reminiscent of some of the German Romantics. One wonders what Schubert would have done with it.

As Louis MacNeice pointed out in a review of Yeats' work, few poets "have been able to write lyrics after thirty-five". The love poems in the transitional volumes of 1904 and 1910 show no sign of a slackening in pace, although they are perhaps a little less dream-laden, offering rather more practical commentary. 'The Folly of Being Comforted' (14 lines, but hardly a sonnet) uses the advice of a well-meaning friend to launch its refusal: "The fire that stirs about her" will not go out. 'Never Give All the Heart', written in despair at the news of Gonne's marriage to John MacBride in 1903, has a touch of Housman about it ("And O 'tis true, 'tis true") but uses couplets to biting effect. 'Red Hanrahan's Song About Ireland' stands out as a powerful and eminently performable lyric which mythologises Yeats' and Maud Gonne's love (she claimed it was her favourite poem of his). She had performed the part of Cathleen ni Houlihan at the Abbey Theatre in Yeats' 1902 verse drama. Biographical detail apart, there are all kinds of symbolic twists and turns in this richly rhetorical piece (the significance of the wind from the left hand, for instance, the Irish unlucky side), emotions veritably howling through the repeated word "Houlihan". It is a poem that spouts passion rather than trickling as some of the lesser lyrics do at this stage.

'Adam's Curse' (1902) is the real surprise in *In the Seven Woods*.

It is as much a poem about the role and task of the poet as it is a love poem, and it cannot really be called a lyric. It moves in dignified rhyming couplets to a very clear-eyed discussion of love. There is no pacing with a personification among the stars. Instead, the mention of past pleasures (and more fire imagery) merely silences the group of companions: "We sat grown quiet at the name of love;/We saw the last embers of daylight die ..." and although there is an upwelling of description, there is no fleeing to hide out in mythological caves. Yeats has a new sense of responsibility.

'No Second Troy' (1908) was composed shortly after the consummation of Willie and Maud's affair, at a time, however, when he was growing mistrustful of her increasingly violent political activities. With its hammered-out questions and its aggressive diction ("ignorant", "hurled", "being what she is") it is much the most plain-spoken of the love poems in *The Green Helmet* and certainly sounds as if the cold wind of reality has caught the poet. The fire imagery that we have commented on in earlier poems is now distant, emblematic ("simple as a fire"), but by the end of the poem it is a potential holocaust. What, indeed, would have happened to Yeats' poetry had they married? The poem has been much praised, although one can see William H. Pritchard's point when he writes that it:

> is all there on the surface, its attitudes fully 'struck', its dramatic posture loud and clear. It works by excluding, by simply not bringing up for consideration anything which might work against the brilliantly contrived sequence of impossible questions it pretends to entertain.

Fire gives way to water in the subsequent lyrics in Yeats' *Collected Poems*. *Responsibilities* has few – the poet has other things to think about. But *The Wild Swans at Coole* opens with what might be his most classically perfect love poem ('The Wild Swans at Coole', 1916) although the famous opening was only achieved after several drafts, starting with: "These woods are in their autumn colours/But the Coole Water is low". After much effort, he came up with the familiar lines: "The trees are in their autumn beauty,/The woodland paths are dry ...". The elegiac note is strong, but there is nothing self-indulgent here: the business-like description sees to that. As always, Yeats' line-breaks are exemplary, "water" reflecting "Mirror" with a metrical inversion like a ruffling to the poem's surface before we settle back to "a still sky". The 'mm' sounds hum with contentment ("Mirrors", "brimming", "among"), and the way the poet keeps himself out of the frame for the time being makes us want to read on: we know that the hero is about to enter: "The nineteenth autumn has come upon me/Since I first made my count." This is not anything like colloquial language, yet the impression is of a plain style. The syntax, the pacing, the tone, are all distinctly conversational, though conversation of the lofty kind Yeats was used to. The individuality is in idiomatic usages: "come upon me", "well finished" and Yeatsian diction – "clamorous". We are not given any explanation as to why he should be counting the swans or what the number fifty-nine signifies, although it's a natural enough thing to do: so many swans together would be impressive. Nor are we asked to view the swans in any heavily symbolic manner ("I would we were changed to white birds on the wandering foam ..."): the emphasis is on capturing the mood of the scene and the latent energy in all those wings. This Yeats achieves once again with his enjambment, internal word-music and strategically placed pauses and stresses: "I saw (*pause*) before (*rhyming echo*) I had well finished (*pause*) /Âll (*echoes "well" and the dark "aw", "ore" vowel of previous line*) sûddenly môunt (*three heavy stresses, then run-on line*) /And scatter (*brittle sound, then pause*), wheeling (*breathy pronunciation of 'wh' suggests wing-beat*) in great broken rings (*three stresses: flapping 'r' sounds: run-on line*)/Upon their clamorous wings. (*shuddering effect of "clamorous", wings/rings rhyme*). No doubt Yeats over-emphasised all this in his public readings, which could seem comical because he wanted to let the free-verse school hear how much trouble he had taken.

We move to the centre-piece of the five stanzas and we begin to see what is on the poet's mind. "All's changed", he tells us, with two heavily stressed words, reminding us of "All suddenly mount". "Brilliant creatures" makes us remember (should we happen to know this) all those women Yeats befriended; perhaps we recollect how vain he was. He is growing old: he was 51 when he wrote this poem. Suddenly, those "great broken rings" of the last stanza recur to us and we realise that they could be representing something more: broken friendships, scattered circles of friends ... Was there even some double meaning in "mount"? The syntax of the last four lines is intricately constructed so that the heavy alliterative footfall of his weariness meets our ears ("Trod with a lighter tread") and contrasts with the skipping "bell-beat of their wings". Having made it clear how counting swans has made him think about the number of his own years, Yeats keeps the focus on the swans, and the fact that traditionally swans have only one mate, one who is "companionable", who prevents them from feeling old and from flying off on fool's errands. The juxtaposition of "cold" with "companionable" perhaps hints at Yeats' doubts about marriage and fidelity; but the word "Attend" in the following lines suggests that he admires and envies the courtliness, the nobility of the swans' lives. After all, they are in Coole Park, Lady Gregory's demesne, where he first spent the summer in 1897, a year of great creative importance to him when he could for a while forget Maud Gonne. At the time of writing this poem, she had been married to and divorced John MacBride, who had just been executed after the Easter Rising. Yeats had proposed marriage yet again and been refused. The poem moves to a tranquil conclusion, but it is an unsettling question that sends us back again to the beginning of the poem to find out what exactly these swans mean to him. Like that enigmatic "Rose" of the early lyrics, the swans have many meanings, but they are real swans, whereas Yeats' roses would not be recognisable to any gardener. It is a tribute to Yeats that he can make a line like "Mysterious, beautiful" succeed without it sounding phoney: certainly he is the last poet who could do so. There is much use of L-sounds in this stanza, lulling us so that we appreciate one aspect of what the poet means when he talks of "awaking". But is he thinking about spiritual possibilities? Death? Missed opportunities? Loss of creativity? Or just waking up to the truth about Maud (how aptly named) Gonne?

There are other love poems in this collection, together with two major tributes to Maud Gonne in 'Her Praise', with its experimental looseness of pentameter and its colloquial note, and 'Broken Dreams'. Yeats' diction is broadening, roughening now: one cannot imagine "some old gaffer" (a beggar, maybe) creeping into any of the *Crossways* poems. Yet Yeats has still not abandoned the high Homeric strain: "From meagre girlhood's putting on/Burdensome beauty". Yeats never lost his affection for his stilts. The elegiac feeling is strong here, but also we sense the poet briefly doubting his own faith in an afterlife – the gentle self-mockery and the attention to the physical reality of his beloved make this one of his most touching love (if not truly lyric) poems. 'A Prayer for My Daughter' (1919) too cannot really be called a lyric, but it is worth mentioning in this context for its subject matter: it is like a medieval book of courtly love, a series of somewhat bizarre hopes and wishes and precepts for his baby daughter. The dramatic opening scene, however, is unforgettable; and the concept of "radical [i.e. rooted] innocence" will become increasingly important to Yeats as he sees Coole and its "accustomed, ceremonious" values disintegrate.

The love poetry of the later Yeats tends to be more dispassionate, more discursive and reflective (see 'Among Schoolchildren') but he never deserts the lyric voice, helped by the viagra-like rejuvenation he experienced in 1934 after his Steinach operation, an "experimental revitalization of the aging puberty gland" (as Frank O'Connor jibed, "like putting a Cadillac engine into a Ford car"). His greatest lyrical outburst, however, was written some years before this, in June 1924, when Yeats was requested a poem by his old friend George Russell and he found himself returning to the swan imagery, but in a very different way. This time the swan is assertively male: Zeus in one of his 'masks'. 'Leda and the Swan' has become a controversial poem because of its portrayal of rape. It probably never was possible to read this sonnet merely as a piece of classical storytelling, but our relatively recent maturity on the subject of rape makes a contemporary reader feel even more uncomfortable. Yet think of what we find tolerable in the cinema. It is heavily erotic, graphic ("A shudder in the loins"), shocking in its brutality – but then, this is meant to be Zeus asserting his godly masculinity and also bringing about the conception of Helen who will go on to set Troy aflame. One can see what appealed to Yeats in this, and he handles the sonnet form masterfully. It is worth remembering, too, how poets tend to view the sonnet as a feminine form – Seamus Heaney has talked about the sonnet's "waist", for example.

The final books of Yeats' *Collected Poems* tend to be more convincing in celebrating the quiet life and the continuing intellectual quest (see 'An Acre of Grass', or the "house, wife, daughter, son" of 'What Then?') than the licentious world of 'Crazy Jane' and the "wild old wicked man", yet every reader can find a gem: 'After Long

Silence' is one, written about Olivia Shakespear, and some from *A Woman Young and Old* (such as 'A Last Confession'). Yeats' *Last Poems* concludes with the 12 short lines of 'Politics' (1938), in which desire is seen as an unavoidable distraction, beauty as a necessary tonic, the only antidote to so-called 'important', 'relevant', 'worldly' club-talk. Yeats chooses to end his life's work with a cry from the heart: "But, O that I were young again/And held her in my arms."

4

Politics and Players: the Public Yeats

Yeats was not always a "smiling public man", and although he was laughed at fairly regularly for his 'mumbo-jumbo', his entanglements with young women and his wealth of eccentricities, there have always been plenty who find nothing to smile about in his political sympathies. George Orwell, for one, felt that "the relationship between Fascism and the literary intelligentsia badly needs investigating, and Yeats might well be the starting-point". It is true that some of the thinking in *A Vision* and his persistent rejection of democratic values can be alarming in retrospect; but it is generally felt that he only (as his son put it) "dabbled" in Fascism. The poet's political convictions and involvements are more labyrinthine than even Orwell can have imagined, but we can fathom something of their depth from the detail Roy Foster has given us in his recent two volume biography. One of the most interesting overviews of Yeats as a public poet, however, comes in a chapter from *Poetry and Experience* (1960) by the American poet Archibald MacLeish, who had much experience in public life as an Assistant Secretary of State under Roosevelt. He anticipates Joseph Campbell when he writes, "Our dreams are public. Even our terrors are public. And nevertheless we won't have our poetry out of doors ..." going on to suggest that "Art *should* do whatever art *can* do. The only question worth considering is whether it can." He then cites the example of Yeats as "the poet who tried most explicitly and most consciously in our time" to show that a sense of public duty is not necessarily "a vice in a poet".

Yeats became a public figure with the success of his early 'Celtic Twilight' writings and his work on founding an Irish National Theatre, but his range of influential friends and his outspoken sympathies for the Fenian cause (particularly through Maud Gonne) ensured that he was someone whose views were asked for and listened to. His power of oratory, honed on gruelling tours round America, could be used to devastating effect, as when he addressed the Oxford Union in 1921 and in a mere seven minutes made it fearlessly apparent what he thought of the way England was treating the Irish. "He was cheered to the echo. The Union had never heard eloquence like that," wrote the undergraduate who had invited him. It seemed all the more powerful to this young Irish student, James O'Reilly, by contrast with the 'other' public Yeats he had seen, some months before, indulging in his role as poet on the steps of his house in Broad Street, Oxford: " … his greying hair blown by the wind, bowing low" and kissing the hand of Lady Ottoline Morrell, then gazing after her "with his open hand above his head in salute. I was not the only passer-by who stopped for a moment or two to watch that performance which I think no one enjoyed more than the poet actor himself." Given this ability to sway and impress in the public arena, it is not surprising that the much-mocked 'Pensioner Yeats' was in 1922 invited to become 'Senator Yeats' in the Dáil of the new Free State.

We have noted before that *Responsibilities* (1914) was the book in which Yeats' work began to reflect his less dreamy, more critical view of the world. The year it was published was, of course, a year in which that world changed utterly. For Yeats and his contemporaries it would be the Easter Rising that had the more lasting impact. The Great War seemed something irrelevant to Irish troubles, as suggested in the well-known poem about Lady Gregory's son, the 'Irish Airman' who 'foresees his death' and which would appear in 1919: "Those that I fight I do not hate,/Those that I guard I do not love …" Yeats would dedicate an even finer poem specifically to Robert Gregory's memory, but he chose to make the dead man here an emblematic figure of the futility of this particular conflict. Yet by making it a monologue and set "in the clouds", with only abstract "tumult", no hint of the mud and guts of the Western Front, the poet was distancing himself. There is no public denunciation of the fighting, nothing like Owen, whose work he disliked and deliberately excluded from his *Oxford Book of Modern Verse*, commenting that "passive suffering is not a theme for poetry" and insisting as only a non-combatant could that "in all the great tragedies, tragedy is a joy to the man who dies ..." Perhaps those men in the trenches would have understood what he meant by the importance of laughter and song, but Yeats' only direct poetic 'statement' on the war (there was also a very oblique 'Meditation') was written in 1915 for an anthology in aid of refugees, 'On Being Asked for a War Poem'.

Before the First World War and before the Easter Rising and subsequent Civil War, Yeats' main battles were with his own family (notably sisters Lolly and Lily and their Cuala Press), with members of the Hermetic Order of the Golden Dawn (he threw Aleister Crowley downstairs) and most publicly, with those involved in the Abbey Theatre. The notion of a national theatre for Ireland grew out of young Yeats' friendship with the middle-aged widow Augusta Gregory of Coole Park: she would be a provider of money but also of ideas and encouragement. Yeats turned to Lady Gregory at every crisis in his life and his correspondence with her is fascinating. She was an enthusiastic folklorist, ambitious to establish a 'salon' on the West Coast, and was to prove a playwright of considerable ability; indeed, her hand can be detected in many of Yeats' own plays. When in 1896 he met J.M. Synge, whose drama would soon cause such a furore among the Dublin middle classes, the scheme began to become a reality and what had begun as an Irish Literary Theatre of myth and 'tapestry' became something more purposeful and controversial. Yeats' aesthetic ideas appear in a key essay, 'The Reform of the Theatre' and he was particularly inspired by the work of Gordon Craig and by F.R. Benson's Shakespeare season in Stratford.

The Irish National Theatre was a project of immense social and political significance. It began in 1902 with a collaboration between Gregory and Yeats which seemed designed to put the case: *Cathleen ni Houlihan*, with Maud Gonne in the title role, a production which (as Stephen Coote points out) "immediately became deeply rooted in the nationalist imagination" and caused one member of the audience (and Yeats himself, in a late poem) to wonder "if such plays should be produced unless one was prepared for people to go out and shoot and be shot". Certainly, the nucleus of the theatre company was highly political, but Yeats was determined that artistic values should not be undermined. His position at the helm was crucial, despite his mask of apparent insensitivity: he was prepared to fight in the public arena to get the very best for Irish audiences. He would not give them the kind of 'agitprop' Maud Gonne seemed to want, but if a well-crafted play was going to shock people, then so be it. The only equivalent in English theatre is the political work of the 1960s. Indicative of how central the theatre would become to political life is the fact that in May 1913, one of the future leaders of the Easter Rising had a play put on at what was now The Abbey Theatre. It was programmed, with uncanny prescience, alongside Tagore's *The Post Office*.

Naturally, the plays Yeats wrote and staged have their own literary merits, but the experience also fed into his verse in several ways, not least in making him more conscious of a listening, critical audience. He does not write directly about the experience very much, but there are heartfelt lines such as those from 'All Things Can Tempt Me' (quoted in the chapter on mythology), his version of Ronsard ('At the Abbey Theatre') and – with specific reference to Synge's iconoclastic work – the squib 'On Those that hated *The Playboy of the Western World,* 1907', whose title is not much shorter than the poem. Many of the songs from Yeats' plays became independent lyrics in subsequent collections and Richard Finneran's 'New Edition' of 1983 added yet more.

At the time of the opening of the Abbey (December 1904), another affair was brewing, one that was to prompt a good deal of 'public' poetry and occupy Yeats for many years to come. Sir Hugh Lane, who was Lady Gregory's nephew, had offered the Dublin Corporation thirty-nine Impressionist paintings but only on the condition that they were given a suitable home – ideally, a splendid new Lutyens gallery spanning the River Liffey. The response was so lukewarm, suspicious and blatantly philistine that he let the National Gallery in London have them instead. When the *Lusitania* was torpedoed in 1915 with Lane on board, it appeared from his will that he wished them to remain in England. However, a pencilled codicil suggested otherwise and Yeats was heavily involved in fighting the case, publicly condemning the reaction of Dublin's ignorant bourgeoisie. As George Moore recollected: "It is impossible to imagine the hatred which came into his voice when he spoke the words 'the middle classes'." The poem Yeats wrote over Christmas and New Year 1912/13 displays some of that hatred and scorn in the part-colloquial, part-oratorical style, in the puffed-out alliteration of its *p*s and *b*s and in the exasperated prolixity of its title, 'To a Wealthy Man Who Promised a Second Subscription to the Dublin Municipal Gallery if it were Proved the People Wanted Pictures'. The 'Wealthy Man' who had suggested nobody wanted an art gallery was the Guinness magnate Lord Ardilaun. In January 1913 Yeats published the poem (as 'The Gift') in the *Irish Times* with a leading article by his future biographer Joseph Hone. It became a focus for the debate and sparked a furious response from the wrong millionaire, but one who was adequately philistine – the anti-Parnellite William Martin Murphy – whose perfectly reasonable suggestion was that he would rather see one decent block of homes at low rents with proper sanitation than "all the pictures Corot and Degas ever painted". Murphy would probably not have realised that the old W.B. Yeats had been keen enough to draw inspiration from 'Paudeen', from beggars and tinkers, but 'To a Wealthy Man …' makes it plain (in thumped out *abab* rhyme) that the new Yeats has different ideas, at least for the moment: art should not have any truck with what "th'onion-sellers thought or did"; great artists need not consult the common people. He would be proved dramatically wrong by a group of ordinary Dubliners before the decade was out and there would have to be yet another W.B. Yeats; but meanwhile, later in 1913, he returned indirectly to the Hugh Lane affair in a more celebrated poem.

The great public theme of Yeats' poetry is the Fenian movement, originally a secret society formed after the catastrophe of the Potato Famine, pledged to expel the British and found a republic. 'Fenian' simply means the Irish. In the 'General Introduction' to his work, Yeats writes: "It was through the old Fenian leader John O'Leary I found my theme" and he is thinking of the Irish heroic legends, but the journalist O'Leary had been imprisoned for four years and exiled for his nationalism. His "voice from the heroic past" (Foster) appealed to Yeats junior as much as to his father and led him to join the Young Ireland Society when he was twenty. But it took many more years for him to find the kind of poetic voice that could write about politics rather than heroic romance. It was O'Leary's name that came to him when he was struggling to express his continuing anger at the Gallery affair. The poem 'September 1913' had in fact been brewing for some weeks and was finished on 9th August while Yeats was in Somerset visiting a medium who had been recommended to him. The directness of approach that he used in the poem to Hugh Lane is even more effective here. O'Leary is consigned to the refrain, but it is significant that he is there at all. The language is not of Faery, of Cuchulain, Emer or Fand; nor of erudition, the Plautus, Guidobaldo, Michelozzo of 'To a Wealthy Man …'; but rather we meet relatively recent, if historical, figures: FitzGerald, Emmet and Tone. Others even less glamorous, even more immediate – "MacDonagh and MacBride/ And Connolly and Pearse" – will come in three years.

The opening lines are defiantly public. "You" is no longer a wealthy patron, and certainly not the "you" of the love poems: it is the people of Dublin and they are being addressed, insulted, harangued from the podium. But at the same time it could be any of us who fumble in a "greasy till", two more words not in Yeats' pre-*Responsibilities* vocabulary. Bitter sarcasm spins "halfpence" and "pence" as it did in 'To a Wealthy Man …' Yeats would no doubt rather be using the word "dream" than "sense", but this is new territory, a new voice: "For men were born to pray and save." Never has sarcasm ('irony' is too subtle a word) been used so effectively in verse, or at least not since Pope invited his readers to pass a day at Timon's villa. It is surprising that Yeats was not lured by the heroic couplet, so well equipped for satire; but he stands by his octosyllabic *ababcdcd* stanzas. Anyone doubting the versatility of W.B. Yeats would do well to set this poem beside one of his earlier love poems and simply compare the effect the rhymes have on us; then ask how does he achieve it. It is to do with diction, syntax, tone, the use of simple conjunctions to suggest the monotony of common life and even the line breaks, marching the poem onward, over the top, recklessly: "What need you, being come to sense,/But fumble in a greasy till/And add the halfpence to the pence/And prayer to shivering prayer, until …"

When it comes to "the names that stilled your childish play", and the implication that somehow 'we' have lost our nerve, Yeats varies the metre to suggest their difference: "They have gone about the world like wind", where the first three syllables are an anapaest. How much more striking than to continue with something iambic such as "They went about the world like wind". By the third stanza, the energy in the speaker has forced the metre briefly into reverse:

"*Was* it for this ...?" and the enjambment suggests the opening of historical perspectives ("spread/the grey wing"). The "delirium of the brave" is Yeatsian rhetoric, but it does not mar the poem, and 'September 1913' even survives its rather sepia-tinted final image as he imagines how we (or contemporary Dubliners) might react to the heroes of the past. This is offered rather in the spirit of those who argue that if Christ returned today the churches would throw him out. We do need to remember that all this "delirium" is about a collection of French paintings and an art gallery, a very provincial affair – albeit one that was becoming highly politicised by the rival claims of London and Dublin. It would not be until Easter, 1916, that Yeats would find a worthier theme and have to eat his words.

'Easter 1916' has been called a 'palinode' to 'September 1913' and it does indeed acknowledge a return to some of the values whose absence he is so bitterly lamenting in the earlier poem. This adds fuel to his own claim that "we make out of the quarrels with others rhetoric, but out of the quarrels with ourselves poetry". Yeats said of the Easter Rising, which occurred while he was in England, that he had no idea "any public event could so deeply move me" and while being a very public poem, his response is also intensely personal as he knew many of the men and women who were involved and several of them were poets. Briefly explained, about seven hundred republicans under the command of Patrick Pearse (a headmaster and poet) occupied Dublin city centre from 24th – 29th April 1916, holding out in the Post Office in O'Connell Street, where the bullet marks can still be seen. Within days, fifteen of the leaders had been executed (and others including his old friend Con Markievicz of Lissadell were imprisoned) at Kilmainham.

The tone of 'Easter 1916' is very different from 'September 1913': it is an elegy for the dead rebels, but also a poem of self-scrutiny. It can be read, too, as "a last, elegiac love lyric to Gonne" (Foster). Yeats turns the mockery of 1913 on himself, telling "a mocking tale or a gibe/To please a companion/Around the fire at the club", and offers us a penitential half-rhyme (*gibe/club*) to make his squirming apparent. For all his haughtiness, for all his querulousness, W.B. Yeats knew when he was wrong and was capable of humility. That so great a public statement is also a display of humble-pie-eating should not perhaps surprise us: the most impressive political speeches have been ones of apology or regret, resignations, abdications, even last words at the scaffold. This is as much an 'elegy for himself' as Chidiock Titchborne's monosyllabic lament from the Tower; but on the surface it mourns the dead men and is stunned by their brutal execution. Lily Yeats wrote that there was "not a vicious man among them except perhaps MacBride", Maud Gonne's ex-husband. Interestingly, Gonne herself disliked 'Easter 1916' because she felt Yeats' mood at the time of writing (September) confused it "till even some of the verses become unintelligible to many".

But for readers today that ambiguity is the fascination of the poem: climbing the mountain, one suddenly finds oneself moving "from cloud to tumbling cloud". What is Yeats saying about these people? He seemed to be praising them, admiring them at first, but now he is implying that their hearts were stone (or might have become stone). He is thinking of his own acquaintances, of Maud Gonne in particular, who remembered him reading her the poem and imploring her to "forget the stone and its inner fire for the flashing, changing joy of life". He is thinking too of his own creative impulse. He knows he must be transformed as a poet, have "the confidence to break moulds" (Foster). But then the poem twists again: we feel the poet grappling with a problem, a mind that instinctively thinks in tessellated images, Byzantine in every sense, forcing itself into rational patterns. The "enchanted" stone is now definitely unwelcome, yet (the poet is obliged to conclude) necessary. 'Heaven' is not often in Yeats' vocabulary; and he is not prepared to judge the actions of the republicans. They were part of his world, common types or not. The snobbishness is hard to keep down, but it has received a severe rebuke. And even that description of the "drunken, vainglorious lout" is justified when we know how abominably MacBride treated Maud and Iseult Gonne. The poem is a 'song' and life up until now has been a 'comedy'. The poet and dramatist in Yeats are both reeling here, trying to reconcile art and life, to be true to the theory that "tragedy is a joy to the man who dies".

What is certain by the end of the poem is that Yeats feels the individuals named have acted heroically, have revived his faith in Irish values. 'Easter 1916' ends in a manner as far from rhetoric as can be imagined. The poet is divided, pulled one way then another: tempted to escape into Celtic twilight, but snapping himself out of it

("No, no …"), questioning repeatedly, leaping in one direction only to land on shaky half-rhymes (*faith/death, enough/love*) but hazarding the hope that Home Rule might after all be granted as promised by the English Parliament. Ironically, all that he can do is fall back on a ceremonial litany of names, something that might be intoned in the Catholic mass, provide some musical effects in the metrical fanfare of "Now and in time to be" and flood the stage with green light, symbolic of Ireland, but also of "the envy in my thought".

Concerned that the poem would get him into trouble (there were already moves afoot to withdraw his Civil List Pension because of perceived German sympathies) Yeats withheld 'Easter 1916', only circulating it among friends. He guessed that many readers would miss its ambiguities and see it as a pro-republican work. It eventually appeared in *The New Statesman* in 1920. There were other poems about the Rising, too, chiefly ballads: 'Sixteen Dead Men', 'The Rose Tree', but also the touching 'On a Political Prisoner', about Yeats' friend of many years, Constance Markievicz (née Gore-Booth), who only narrowly escaped execution. Yeats wrote, too, about the more conventionally heroic Roger Casement: he had been collaborating with Germans to raise support for the rebellion, but there was strong feeling about the case right up to his execution in August. Con's sister Eva (the "two beautiful figures among the trees at Lissadell") had asked Yeats to intercede.

In Yeats' later poems, there is no less weight given to political concerns, and there are many ballad-style commentaries ('The Ghost of Roger Casement', 'Come Gather Round Me Parnellites') sometimes taking a broad perspective as in 'The Curse of Cromwell' with its despairing refrain. Yeats looks back but also anticipates an equally famous political balladeer of future years who will cry "the times they are a'changing".

His inclination to brevity leads to some inspired political squibs (see the chapter on epigrams) and there are inevitably coded references to key events, such as Kevin O'Higgins' assassination in 1927. But Yeats is generally much more sceptical, more wary and politics never again take centre stage. On a practical level, however, he did become briefly involved with social reform as a Senator of the new Free State, visiting educational institutions in his official capacity, perhaps recalling Pearse's words that "we can bring the heroes and seers and scholars to the schools and get them to talk to the children". One of his best late poems, 'Among Schoolchildren', was stimulated by one such visit in 1916 to St Otteran's School. It is a meditation on loss and change and, of course, Maud Gonne: "I look upon one child or t'other there/And wonder if she stood so at that age – ", but has its own wry observations on society too: "The children learn to cipher and to sing;/To study reading-books and history,/To cut and sew, be neat in everything/In the best modern way ..."

Beyond the schoolroom, Yeats had learned that it was safer in the new Ireland not to indulge too much in political commentary and anyway was more inclined to agree with Michael Robartes that "opinion is not worth a rush". During the Civil War and the rash of assassinations and reprisal killings that accompanied it, the poet had retreated into his new home, the restored keep, Thoor Ballylee. He employs local references rather than confronting events in a way that might interest *The Irish Times.* The sequences, 'Nineteen Hundred and Nineteen' and its companion 'Meditations in Time of Civil War' (1921-22) are just that: meditations, structured symphonically, despite their creator's appalling ear for music, and among his finest achievements. In the latter poem, for example, we do not hear about the bridge beside Yeats' tower being blown up (which it was – the explosion was heard sixteen miles away) but we meet one of the characters who might have done it: "An affable Irregular,/A heavily-built Falstaffian man,/Comes cracking jokes of civil war ...", together with his opposite, the Lieutenant, "Half dressed in national uniform". In *Object Lessons,* Eavan Boland comments on how this fifth section "takes a public reality of fixed meaning – a civil war fought in a rural setting – and destabilizes it through the intensity of a private world." Yeats is more concerned now with questions of inheritance and the philosophical significance of violence than with politics, musing on the paradox of tranquil demesnes created by "violent, bitter men". 'Nineteen Hundred and Nineteen' is also more elegy than polemic, putting the current crisis into a perspective reaching back to Ancient Greece and the sculptor, Phidias. In the opening stanzas, Yeats reflects on his own shaken optimism; he only sees "dragon-ridden days" now, and despite the reassurance of the swan/soul comparison in Section III (the 'slow movement' of this symphony), his bitterness returns in sharp epigrammatic form in IV (the 'scherzo'), which precedes an exhortation to "mock at the great" and a vision of ceaseless "Violence upon the roads". We feel that the poet has a new understanding of how impossible it is to control events, to manipulate the progress of the future: life has to run freely like the waters racing under his window in a later poem, 'Coole and Ballylee, 1931'. 'Meditations in Time of Civil War', although similar in its symphonic structure to 'Nineteen Hundred and Nineteen', focuses more on the tower itself, enduring in "this tumultuous spot" through other "long wars"; on an ancient Japanese sword given to Yeats after a lecture, suggesting how one may stay bright and sharp and yet be safely tucked in a scabbard; and on the richly symbolic, yet genuinely observed "stare's (*starling's*) nest by my window":

> The bees build in the crevices
> Of loosening masonry, and there
> The mother birds bring grubs and flies.
> My wall is loosening; honey-bees,
> Come build in the empty house of the stare ...

Yeats knew that his creativity was the most precious thing in his life and felt that he had much more still to say. Even if the 'masonry' of society was falling about him, even if he had lost his "bee-loud glade", he must go on making honey.

5

Up the Winding Stair: Yeats the Occultist

We have already touched on some of Yeats' occult interests and suggested that they were a natural progression from his explorations of 'Faeryland' and Celtic myth. But he had been attracted to spiritualism from an early age, through the yarns of his uncle George Pollexfen, and began exploring Theosophy with his school friend Charles Johnston, then at the Dublin Hermetic Society in his late teens. The effect of hearing the mystic Mohini Chatterjee speak there and "set at rest/A boy's turbulent days" was still powerful enough in 1928 to inspire a poem for *The Winding Stair.* His friend from art school, George Russell (the poet AE), was another liberating influence, although more inclined to mysticism than magic, and he became more sceptical and sardonic as he grew older. At this age, Yeats himself was wary; and after attending a séance with Katharine Tynan in 1888 where he was afflicted with convulsions and inexplicable visions, he resolved not to try anything like it again. He wrote later how he often asked himself "what was that violent impulse that had run through my nerves. Was it a part of myself – something always to be a danger perhaps; or had it come from without, as it seemed?"

Yeats' resolution of 1888 did not last long and as he became more famous, so he was able to visit more mediums. In May 1912 he acquired a 'spirit guide', Leo Africanus: "I get the presence of living independent minds gathering together" to "plunge into our world like seabirds," he wrote in a notebook. These activities reached a peak in the years leading up to the First World War, a period which saw a surge of interest in voices from the afterlife. The physicist Sir Oliver Lodge's *Raymond*, about his son who had died in the trenches, was just one of the more popular books on the subject read by Yeats. But there was also Swedenborg and Plotinus. It was not until he was in his fifties that the occult moved to the centre of Yeats' creative work and it would take even longer for him to find a way of moulding it into satisfactory poetry. The source was the automatic writing produced by his young wife, George, whom he had unexpectedly married in 1917. In the first days of the marriage it looked as though it was going to be the disaster many of Yeats' friends could have predicted. He had only just proposed to Maud Gonne and then her daughter, Iseult, to whom he was writing intimate, worried notes while on his honeymoon. As Brenda Maddox puts it in *George's Ghosts*, the best account of their relationship, "Yeats' friends laughed. There was something Chaucerian about an ageing bachelor marrying a much younger woman" (and an ageing bachelor, she might have added, who displayed his beloved Kelmscott Chaucer on its lectern in his home).

The poet's reaction to marriage was an attack of fever and an overpowering "dread" of "some accidental revelation". The revelation would be of a quite different order, and occurred a week after the wedding, when George must have been only too cruelly aware of what faced her. It is not surprising that biographers such as Maddox have seen George's "miraculous intervention" as a cry for help and her offerings of raw material a device to keep this elderly philanderer excited and at home. A more romantic interpretation of it can be found in Yeats' allegorical long poem, 'The Gift of Harun Al-Rashid' (1923) in which "Truths without father came, truths that no book/Of all the uncounted books that I have read,/Nor thought out of her mind or mine begot". The new husband wrote to Lady Gregory from their honeymoon hotel in Ashdown Forest: "She got a piece of paper, & talking to me all the while so that her thoughts would not effect what she wrote, wrote these words (which she did not understand) 'with the bird' (Iseult) 'all is well at heart ...'" going on to explain how suddenly his aches and pains vanished and "From being more miserable than I ever remember being since Maud Gonne's marriage I became extremely happy." And so he remained; and so began the automatic writing and what would become *A Vision* in 1925.

The Wild Swans at Coole is the first collection to show evidence of this new excitement. 'Ego Dominus Tuus' was composed some years before, but suggests his readiness for seeding. The mouthpiece *Ille* (or 'Willy' as Pound quipped) is "enthralled by the unconquerable delusion,/Magical shapes." "*Ille*. By the help of an image/I call to my own opposite, summon all/That I have handled least, least looked upon …" What the poet had truly "handled least", the "old iron, old bones, old rags", would not appear in his verse for some years. At this stage, it is the occult that calls him, and Georgie Hyde-Lees was indeed in many ways his 'opposite'. Although 'The Double Vision of Michael Robartes' (1919) has an authority and a latent energy that anticipates 'The Second Coming' ("I suddenly saw/A Sphinx with woman breast and lion paw …"), some of the first 'visionary' poems are too self-conscious, too eager to present the 'system'. This was not only emerging from George's automatic writing, but being distilled by Yeats from decades of esoteric study. Robartes' speech, 'Twenty-and-eight the phases of the moon …' from 'The Phases of the Moon' (1918) is often quoted to demonstrate the poet's ideas about cycles of human civilization, but it is a poem of more interest to biographers and critics than poetry readers. The same might be said for *A Vision*, although Foster echoes the spirits themselves ("we come to give you metaphors for poetry") when he reminds us that its rationale is "a factory for mysterious images assembled into great poems" and Kathleen Raine finds clarity in it. "For mysticism is not synonymous with vagueness, subjectivity and emotion," she writes in *Defending Ancient Springs*: "it is, on the contrary (as Yeats points out in his introduction to *A Vision*), characterized by an 'arbitrary, harsh, and difficult symbolism'". Certainly, by the time Yeats was completing it he was "longing to put it out of reach" and to write the poems it was making possible.

'The Second Coming' (January 1919) is one such, catching the mood of revelation which the poet felt in those early spiritualist sessions with his wife at Ashdown, Glendalough and Oxford. The poem's reference to '*Spiritus Mundi*' reminds us how attuned much of his work is to that of C.G. Jung, whose 'collective unconscious' has many parallels with Yeats' "general storehouse of images"(just as the psychoanalyst's 'archetypes' link with Yeats' phases of the moon). But it is the energy of 'The Second Coming' that is so arresting: the metre of "Turning and turning" has a heavy, centrifugal out-thrust to it; "widening" is a long-drawn-out sound, made even more so by the 'i' of "gyre" (which, sadly, is meant to be pronounced with a hard 'g': see Chapter 10 for more on gyre theory). The relaxed iambs and the echoing space between the 'fs' of "The falcon cannot hear the falconer" are like a general pause between dramatic dissonances in music. Suddenly "Things fall apart" (*pause*) "the centre cannot hold" (*pause*); "Mere anarchy is loosed upon the world", where "mere" means 'pure'. What would the effect of 'pure' have been? There is a snarling, searing note to "mere" that Yeats must have liked. The poem becomes a list of catastrophic changes, offset by the vision in the second half, which the poet does not try to interpret. He presents us with the vision and the puzzle of the "rough beast" heading towards Bethlehem, leaves us to ask ourselves: is this history, or history repeating itself? The power of 'The Second Coming' is the power of a dream which makes 'no sense' but is so compelling that we do not want to wake up from it. Or it is like an expressionist painting that shocks with its violent imagery, but does not explain itself. This is the most extreme and most successful of visionary Yeats, but it is, to a certain extent, a dead end. He would have to work hard to find a 'repeatable' method of expressing his vision and a fitting retort to Lady Gregory's remark: "He hasn't done much work since his marriage".

The Winding Stair and Other Poems (1933) is perhaps Yeats' finest collection. The bitter preoccupations with youth, age and inheritance which dominated *The Tower* now play cello, viola and second fiddle to the sweeter theme George has helped him to perfect ("as above, so below"). The final poem in the 1928 book had been the *Epilogue to 'A Vision'*, 'All Souls' Night', which prepares us for what is to come ("Because I have a marvellous thing to say/A certain marvellous thing/None but the living mock ...") although it lapses into a rather rambling sequence of remembered names from his spiritualist questing. The first poem in the collection of 1933 is the elegy for the aristocrat-cum-revolutionaries Eva Gore-Booth and Con Markievicz, a tender erotic reminiscence barbed with images from the Easter Rising, innocence confronting experience. The fight for Home Rule is in the past; Yeats is a Senator of the Free State, and he is implying that so much of the struggle for it was "folly", that the girls' beauty was more precious, that time is the only enemy and "the fragile structure of Ascendancy achievement" (Foster) is a highly flammable "gazebo", gone in a flash. 'Death', the twelve-line poem that follows, makes the point more economically, in the pompous language of the courts: "A great man in his pride/Confronting murderous men/Casts derision upon/Supersession of breath". Yeats has thus paved the way for his offering, his alternative, which is considered (in a poem originally titled simply 'Sword and Tower') by 'Self' and firstly by 'Soul'. Just as *Ille* did, the poet's 'Soul' makes an invocation, shaping the imagery of Thoor Ballylee ("Ballyphallus" as Pound called it) into a personal mythology, inviting the poet to climb the stairway and escape. The significance of "the star" and "that quarter" lies in Yeats' 'system' and such details might make this poem appear daunting. But the ideas in it about rebirth have been digested and the poet is ready to speak of them without obfuscation, or abstraction, in a plainspoken brace octave (*abbacddc*). Encouragingly, too, 'My Self' replies with a tangible emblem: the ceremonial sword Yeats had been given in Chicago by Junzo Sato, "a very distinguished looking Japanese" and passionate fan of his. Yeats was increasingly drawn to Japanese culture, the mask and ritual of Noh plays, and to certain elements of Buddhism. Sato insisted that the poet accept the sword, which "had been for 500 years in the family". As in 'Meditations in Time of Civil War', this sword is a symbol for the potential creativity of the human soul, but 'My Soul' here is scornful of "wandering/To this and that and t'other thing" and considers life "a crime" by comparison with "ancestral night": it encourages the poet to grow beyond such actions and attain more mystical heights.

But thankfully for readers who feel happier on earth (as Robert Frost said, it's "the right place for love") the poet is not tempted, and in Part II (given over entirely to the 'Self'), there is a feeling of resignation; the lines seem to shrug in the face of inevitability and the result is a curious and unexpected joy: "A living man is blind and drinks his drop./What matter if the ditches are impure ...?" the 'Self' begins, practising its role as rag-and-bone man. All this can be explained philosophically in relation to Yeats' system of beliefs, but it does not need to be and is all the more effective for its lack of names and learned references. The poet simply mentions "enemies" and "a proud woman"; we are not ensnared in autobiography. There is an ease of lyricism, an innocence of tone that (like his master, Blake) just avoids sentimentality. There is even a gaiety that is close to humour: "I am content to follow to its source/Every event in action or in thought;/Measure the lot; forgive myself the lot!"

The Winding Stair is rich in poems of balance, of acceptance. "The swordsman throughout repudiates the saint," Yeats told his first lover, Olivia Shakespear, "but not without vacillation".

'Vacillation' is the title of a key sequence in this book. It is placed shortly after the homage to Chatterjee and the second Byzantium poem, which we shall examine shortly. Yeats prided himself on the "variety of pace" he was achieving in his sequences, and although he had no ear for music (except the psaltery, which he liked to perform to) there is here a quasi-symphonic, rather Mahlerian, structure, as there had been in the Civil War poems. The eight separate sections were composed and combined from 1931 to 1932, opening with the statement of the Blakean theme that we necessarily live "between extremities", and asking the question: "What is joy?" The second 'movement' uses a myth from the Mabinogion and *The Golden Bough*'s favourite fertility god, Attis, to suggest rebirth through the combination of opposites; but the tree is such an archetype, and the idea of a 'burning bush' so familiar, that the lines barely need any gloss and their true power erupts from some deeper stratum within us. Yeats strikes a very Metaphysical note in his writing here, reminding us of his fondness for John Donne. Part III is more informal, opening (and echoing Wordsworth) with "Get" – but the "gold and silver" we are advised to invest in is, of course, the apples of the sun and moon, not money (forgetting for the moment the poet's reaction to hearing he had won the Nobel Prize: *how much?*). Again, there is a touch of humour, some self-mockery ("Lethean foliage") and, to end, some casually shocking sentiments in a brazen C major: "And call those works extravagance of breath/That are not suited for such men as come/Proud, open-eyed and laughing to the tomb." Section IV is a brief scherzo, vivid and moving: an epiphany. Unlike the occasion in London which inspired him to escape to 'The Lake Isle of Innisfree', Yeats now has the confidence to stay in the shop with his teacup, to 'keep his camera running', as it were: "While on the shop and street I gazed/My body of a sudden blazed". The next section is again short, but in a minor key: the word-music is heavy, slow ("storm-scattered intricacy"): two stanzas, each of one sentence in which the final clause is crucial. "Responsibility so weighs me down" is the first; the second, following the weighty trudge of memory through "Things said or done long years ago" is "My conscience or my vanity appalled."

The poet is not overwhelmed by his 'ghost theory' in 'Vacillation'; it has been an airy presence and remains so in Section VI. If this were music, it would be a march, with bells and chorus and the repeated "Let all things pass away" like the three hammer-blows in Mahler's Sixth Symphony. It is a cry to the spirit-world but it does not forget that most poetry readers live in this world. Only in the seventh 'movement' do the years of work on *A Vision* surface – but without any fuss, just six lines of dialogue between 'Heart and Soul' (the original title of the cycle), with 'Heart' claiming the last word: "What theme had Homer but original sin?" – in other words, life has proved itself the most inspiring thing to write about, so any other 'reality', any 'salvation' that excludes unbaptised Homer is not one for Yeats. This marvellous 'symphony' ends quietly, with a reminder of the home key – the theme of 'vacillation' – an affectionate, candid, conversational address to the theologian Baron Friederich von Hügel. Yeats is deliberately (and touchingly) vague about the scriptural reference and his last line is delightfully human, which is perhaps the whole point.

Yeats' occult studies have enabled him to find greater humanity in his writing. But they also opened up a new seam of rhetoric, which he explores to the full in 'Byzantium', a companion piece to 'Sailing to Byzantium'. Here, there is no sitting with a tea-cup in a London shop: we are in the poet's equivalent to Blake's Jerusalem, where language is rich and strange, and the lines of verse wax and wane. Yeats is working in an entirely different medium. If 'Vacillation' makes one think of symphonic music, 'Byzantium' is sculpture, beaten out by "the golden smithies of the Emperor". And yet, ironically, it is the music of the poem that makes it so memorable: the repetitions and echoes are rich and intricate (John Unterecker points out that 35 of the last stanza's 45 words appear at least twice in the poem). Even if one never decides what "that dolphin-torn, that gong-tormented sea" actually *is*, the words leap in one's memory for ever. And lines such as "For Hades' bobbin bound in mummy-cloth/May unwind the winding path" are a joy to run over the tongue, whatever they mean. Of course, the joy of repeating meaningless musical lines is short-lived as the case of Swinburne proves. Whether 'Byzantium' is saying important things about Yeats' theory of gyres; how far we wish to read it as a description of the final purifying dance of spirits before they are reborn; whether we find the network of symbolism is coherent and significant – all this will depend on the individual reader. To this reader, what 'Byzantium' means is that there is a world to which all artists should aspire, where the trivialities of daily life are put in perspective. It may once have existed, may still exist. The historical Byzantium, in Yeats' mind, was a place where "religious, aesthetic and practical life were one" where "architect and artificers … spoke to the multitude and the few alike". But it was also, as Roy Foster puts it, "a gleaming personal emblem". Access to this world of dance and mosaic may be through death, through spiritualism, through imagination or simply through contemplation of a timeless work of art, but it solves "all mere complexities,/The fury and the mire of human veins".

6

Gregorian Chant: Yeats the Elegist

In 1925, Yeats' wife, George, whose automatic writing had inspired so much of his best work, wrote to her friend: "there's nothing in his verse worth preserving but the personal. All the pseudo-mystico-intellecto-nationalistico stuff of the last 15 years isn't worth a trouser-button." While it is surprising to hear this from the *fons et origo* of *A Vision*, there have been many who would agree. Yeats himself, however, insisted: "all that is personal soon rots; it must be packed in ice or salt". This ability to make the personal timeless ("ancient salt is best packing" he added) has impressed generations of readers since George made her throwaway remark. While the love poems are superb of their kind, with an elegy such as 'In Memory of Major Robert Gregory' (1918) Yeats takes his stylistic ambitions to a new level. Frank Kermode (in *Romantic Image*) considers it:

> [the first work ...] in which we hear the full range of the poet's voice ... After it, for twenty years, Yeats' poems, whenever he is using his whole range, are identifiable as the work of the master of the Gregory elegy.

There is little disagreement with Kermode about the quality of those poems in which his friendships are placed in a historical and cultural context: the elegies.

Elegy is a mainstay of English verse, continually revived and re-engineered from Henry King and Milton, through Gray, Wordsworth, Shelley, Tennyson, Arnold, right up to Douglas Dunn's *Elegies* (1985) and Thom Gunn's *The Man With Night Sweats* (1992). From an early age, Yeats had shown himself equipped to join this distinguished company. The elegiac note creeps into poems from the 1890s, such as 'When You are Old', 'The Lamentation of the Old Pensioner', 'He Hears the Cry of the Sedge' and it dominates much of the later work. "Man is in love and loves what vanishes,/What more is there to say?" (from 'Nineteen Hundred and Nineteen') neatly summarises his feelings. But there is a handful of late elegies that are masterpieces and I wish to concentrate on four of these in this chapter. They all have strong associations with Lady Gregory, reflecting the change in Yeats' relationship with her after his marriage, her son's death in action, her own decline and the subsequent loss of Coole (it was eventually razed to the ground in 1941). 'In Memory of Major Robert Gregory' is the first to consider; then 'Coole Park, 1929' and 'Coole and Ballylee, 1931'(sometimes titled 'Coole Park and Ballylee' and originally dated 1932), followed by 'The Municipal Gallery Revisited'.

W.H. Auden's 'In Memory of W.B. Yeats'(1939), is one of the twentieth century's great elegiac poems and in writing it Auden is acknowledging how much his master had made possible within the genre. Yeats was able to "follow right/To the bottom of the night" and "Still persuade us to rejoice ..." Something of this emerges in the Gregory elegy, perhaps because Yeats was never particularly close to his dear friend's son and indeed there was a good deal of resentment from her daughter-in-law. Yeats had, after all, installed himself at Coole as writer-in-residence, occupying the master bedroom and the most important seat at dinner, where he would be encouraged by Augusta to drink the cellar's best wine. Robert was not sympathetic to the nationalist cause, was something of a dilettante and his paintings did not make much impression on Yeats (although his sepia drawing of Thoor Ballylee must surely have appealed). Yet when his death was announced in a note from Lady Gregory in February 1918, and she hinted in a postscript "If you feel like it some time – write something down that we may keep", he had to find a way of commemorating this man.

The best elegies are not always about intimate friends: this was probably the case with Milton's 'Lycidas' and certainly so with Shelley's 'Adonais'. That Robert Gregory was not really a kindred spirit enabled Yeats to mould his image into the 'epitome' that suited him. The "intensity and crystallisation" that Lady Gregory thought he could bring to such an elegy were, did she but know it, the result of his cool (and of course his 'Coole') feelings. He could see Robert Gregory as part of a mosaic, stylised out of all recognition. At least, that is what happens in 'An Irish Airman Foresees His Death', which does not suggest the real man at all: Robert Gregory had, after all, willingly volunteered. Then in Yeats' next attempt, 'Shepherd and Goatherd', the airman is made into a character from a pastoral, a scholar-gipsy who "had thrown the crook away/And died in the great war beyond the sea". These were not quite what Lady Gregory and her somewhat touchy daughter-in-law, Margaret, required and it is usually thought that they both had a hand in guiding Yeats towards appropriate material for the elegy. Yeats writes in letters of "compromise" and resisting their calls for "suggested eloquence about aero planes".

It is not known how these two formidable ladies felt at Yeats' decision to wait until halfway through the poem before mentioning its subject. The Coole Estate is omnipresent, however, and 'In Memory of Major Robert Gregory' is the first Yeats poem to feature Thoor Ballylee. It begins (as if in defiance of George) with 'the personal', but not the death of Robert: rather, a very intimate and perceptive glimpse of the way newly-weds fight over their sets of friends, leading to a sudden, unexpected statement of the main theme: " ... But not a friend that I would bring/This night can set us quarrelling,/For all that come into my mind are dead." This is an arresting way to start the poem, lulling us in the most innocent of language "beside a fire of turf" that will later become "the entire combustible world", taking us up "the narrow winding stair to bed" as if to prepare us for "all lovely intricacies" of the subsequent stanzas. Using an eight-line stanza taken from Cowley (*aabbcddc*), Yeats begins to list the friends he recalls, letting the opening couplets make indelible cameos of his friends ("Lionel Johnson comes the first to mind/That loved his learning better than mankind") while developing broader ideas in each final quatrain. The metre is not fanatically strict and Yeats is content to squeeze in extra stresses and syllables, obedient to Ezra Pound's advice that poets should follow their ears. So the first stanza ends with "All, all are in my thoughts tonight being dead" (at least five stresses) while the fourth: "Passionate and simple like his heart" (not much more than three).

It is Yeats the dramatist who knows that there is sense in keeping your hero offstage for as long as possible. Robert walks on in the sixth stanza just as Yeats has consigned Johnson, Synge, George Pollexfen to "some old picture-book". The impression is of a series of painted curtains being flown to finally reveal a living figure: "Our Sidney and our perfect man". This introduction of Robert in the costume of Sir Philip Sidney is just one of several potentially clumsy moments in the poem, which Yvor Winters made much of ("I confess that I think it is a very bad poem"). But once we recognise the Renaissance costume, the confusion vanishes and the appellation in fact clarifies the portrayal of the dead man as "Soldier, Scholar, Horseman", one who blended qualities which Johnson, Synge and Pollexfen only possessed singly. Besides, the reader is more likely to be struck by the superb line that follows, describing death as a "discourtesy".

The evocation of Coole owes much to Lady Gregory, who adored trees (now "storm-broken"), and to Yeats' own feelings about his new home, the idea of Robert as "your heartiest welcomer" sounding somewhat dutiful. Yet the picture of the vigorous horseman never fails to catch fire in the reader's imagination, even if the anecdotes have something of the feeling of those stories people come up with when remembering friends at a funeral service. Stephen Coote points to the ambiguity in Yeats' choice of verb when he writes: "We dreamed that a great artist had been born/To cold Clare rock and Galway rock and thorn". It is convenient for the poet to say this and its repetitions ("rock … rock", then the introduction of the refrain) catch the ear and touch the heart, but it is Yeats on his stilts, on his 'high horse', mythologizing.

The poem moves steadily towards its climax in the eleventh stanza, with its pronouncement (in close clusters of stresses, bound like the very bundles he is describing) on the options for the Romantic artist: "Some burn damp faggots, others may consume/The entire combustible world in one small room/As though dried straw …" The imagery owes something to Donne ("and makes one little roome an every where"), but the enjambment, the metrical fuse that burns through to "dried straw" and the third appearance of the refrain together make a powerful music:

... and if we turn about
The bare chimney is gone black out
Because the work had finished in that flare.
Soldier, scholar, horseman, he,
As 'twere all life's epitome.
What made us dream that he could comb grey hair?

Pound cannot have approved of "as 'twere" any more than F.W. Bateson did of the last line ("What was he, a barber?") but it is easy to mock Yeats: the achievement here is to write in the high elegiac vein and sustain it – or almost, since the elegy ends rather abruptly with a not altogether convincing excuse reminiscent of Mark Antony's when he breaks off from his tribute to Caesar.

'Coole Park, 1929' and 'Coole and Ballylee, 1931' appear side by side in *The Winding Stair and Other Poems.* The elegiac tone is common to both and each was considered as a possible preface to the book Lady Gregory wrote about Coole in her declining years. She must have sensed that the house would eventually vanish, for Margaret had already persuaded her to sell it to the Forestry Department, who allowed her to remain there until her death. Yeats too foresaw the end of the house itself and it was in fact the 1929 poem with its evocation of nettles waving from a "shapeless mound" that introduced his friend's book, *Coole.* Yeats did not live to see his prophecy come true, but Seamus Heaney, born in the year of Yeats' death, made a short television film in which he walked about those same mounds and broken stone reciting lines from 'Coole Park, 1929'.

It is a rich poem: four stanzas composed (like the other Coole poem and 'The Municipal Gallery Revisited') in *ottava rima*, one of the most versatile of forms, capable of expressing serious emotions without losing the light, conversational touch (it was, remember, Byron's choice for *Don Juan*). He uses half-rhymes to avoid the difficulty of having to find so many similar sounds in each stanza and always manages to keep the right balance between himself, the surroundings and the history they conjure. Yeats – conscious perhaps of the poem's introductory role – never lapses into obscurity. There are hints of symbolism in the "luminous" cloud in the west; the "aged woman" is not named, but this is hardly Cathleen ni Houlihan. Nor are we in Byzantium, yet the walls beget "a dance-like glory" not unlike that Yeats will capture a year later in the poem 'Byzantium'. The poet himself is very much present, from that opening image, "I meditate upon a swallow's flight", to the veiled self-portrait in the second stanza as "one that ruffled in a manly pose/For all his timid heart" but he does not overwhelm it. Other people are his concern. As in the Gregory elegy, the friends whose "glory" he will praise in 'The Municipal Gallery Revisited', are sketched in miniature. Yeats was the son of an artist, the brother of an artist and had attended art school: the desire to capture a likeness was bred into him, but 'portraits' were also associated with the house at Coole. Yeats recalled later seeing a visitor to the house the day after Lady Gregory's death, "a queer Dublin sculptor" looking "at the mezzotints and engravings of ... Fox, Burke and so on, and after standing silent said 'all the nobility of the earth'." So, Synge (one of the mighty Abbey triumvirate) is "that slow man,/That meditative man", as the heaviness of the rhythms suggests. And Lady Gregory's two nephews, John Shawe-Taylor and Hugh Lane, are "Impetuous men" who "Found pride established in humility,/A scene well set and excellent company." But it is the swallow image that attracts Yeats as he is drawn to the 'emblem' of the swan in the companion poem. The intellectuals and artists, like Bede's sparrow in the feasting hall, "came like swallows and like swallows went". They gathered in Augusta Gregory's 'salon' and were wholly dependent for their guidance upon her "compass-point". Her encouragement (and her wealth) gave "certainty" to their "dreaming", even if it meant challenging the establishment and contemporary mores ("That cut through time or cross it withershins") and gaining a reputation as a trouble-maker. Yeats' use of "withershins" suggests going against the natural movement of the sun, just as the final stanza asks a select band of visitors in later years to turn their backs "upon the brightness of the sun" as they remember Lady Gregory's "laurelled head". But he also advises them to avoid "all the sensuality of the shade". The picture conjured is very much in keeping with the famous photograph of Augusta Gregory beneath her catalpa tree in 1927.

'Coole and Ballylee, 1931' is one of the best poems W.B. Yeats wrote. It opens like a computer-generated title sequence, with the bold close-up effect of the stressed first syllables ("Under ... Otters ... Run ..."), zooming through the window of the poet's tower, over the humble window ledge to bob in the water, down into the quotation marks "through 'dark' Raftery's 'cellar'" to the calm, spreading, mildly mocking conclusion ("finish up...drop into a hole ...") The symbolic association is mentioned in the lightest possible manner ("What's water but the generated soul?") as if we couldn't possibly disagree or are expected to smile, yet this is a shrug in the face of death and burial. Lady Gregory had not yet died when he composed the lines beginning: "We were the last romantics ..." but they could have been her epitaph. However, just as was the case in the overall architecture of the Robert Gregory elegy, Yeats holds back from introducing his chief guest until halfway through the poem, after his unsurpassed evocation of the Coole woods (and this from a poet who is supposed to have been fairly indifferent to the natural world), "Now all dry sticks under a wintry sun" and the conceit of Nature as an Elizabethan actor personifying autumn. The change of seasons is seen as an allegory, and such change is "rant" compared to the true poetry of the spirit – the "sudden thunder of the mounting swan": Zeus or Prospero reminding his audience who is in control. Although there is something highly stylised, very heraldic here, as in the third stanza's knowing conceit about "a spot of ink", the poem succeeds because the poet's tone is so genuine and heartfelt, the rhymes and line-breaks shaped with such precision understanding of their effect.

One of the few recordings of Yeats reading his own work features the third and fourth stanzas of this poem. The arrival of Lady Gregory is hurled at the microphone in the familiar chant, almost a monotone, almost out of breath by the end of its long sentence. "Sound of a stick ..." is, of course, supposed to change the mood. We cut cinematically from the "dry sticks" round the lake to a close-up of the occupant's walking stick. But she is virtually lost in her own collection, nameless among the books and heads and pictures, "a last inheritor/Where none has reigned that lacked a name and fame/ Or out of folly into folly came" – sentiments there can be little reason for us to sympathise with, yet the effect is potent, not least because of those obsessive 'a' sounds.

We shall discuss Yeats' gift for the epigrammatic in the next chapter, but it is important to note that this poem's success depends as much on the epigrammatic as it does on the broad arc of its structure. Despite his reputation as a difficult, esoteric poet, Yeats has the gift of finding words for common experiences. No one forgets "We were the last romantics", but even the phrase "Like some poor Arab tribesman and his tent" has become shorthand for the state of homelessness. Perhaps one should say 'Homerlessness', as this is what preoccupies the poet in the closing lines. The passing of Augusta Gregory and the loss of Coole mark the end of the possibility of a grand style. He recognises this and, in lines which manage to transcend their mixture of images, can only look to the swan for inspiration as it: " ... drifts upon a darkening flood."

The last lines of 'The Municipal Gallery Revisited' (1937) are also celebrated for the way they so neatly encapsulate "what oft was thought":

> Think where man's glory most begins and ends
> And say my glory was I had such friends.

This is the true elegiac note – the one that does not sound out of place in the pulpit at a memorial service. Yeats was always comfortable in the company of the dead, shocking Margaret Gregory by insisting on sitting all night with her mother-in-law's body rather than dispatching it to an undertaker's. The dead in this poem are only portraits, but each one lives in Yeats' imagination: they are the swallows about his own compass-point now. The poet is not only revisiting the controversial art gallery but returning to many of his favourite images and themes in a Richard Straussian montage, a 'Heldenleben' of autobiographical snatches and elegiac reverie. Key words recur: the poem could almost be pieced together from these tesserae – "soul", "remorse", "terrible and gay", "pride", "honour", "deep-rooted", "dream" and, of course, "friends". At times, he seems to be paralysed by his own obsessive-compulsive diction, repeating "heart", "cover"; "had looked", "permanent", "son" in the first five lines of the third stanza.

The poem (drafted in prose, then one stanza completed each day) is in many ways, as Roy Foster suggests, a "courtly praise-poem", an elegy for lost Ascendancy values, "a reunion between the poet and the noble dead". Foster is obviously not persuaded by the poem's suggestion that "Coole was apparently better off tumbled to the ground than inhabited by inferiors", calling it "WBY at his most exclusive". It is true that 'The Municipal Gallery Revisited' does not open to the universal in the way that 'Coole and Ballylee, 1931' does and it is hampered as the Gregory elegy was by the poet's awareness that this was 'expected' (he had publicly promised a new poem at an Irish Academy dinner given in his honour). The public elegy is inevitably a compromise, if not with the facts then with the poet's own feelings. For Foster, the last lines "ring hollow" because Yeats knew full well that his "glory" was in his literary reputation. Yes, it is a rhetorical flourish, but it is the expression of a feeling induced by seeing these particular paintings at that particular time in his life, only just over a year before his own death. His prose account of the experience suggests that it was anything but "hollow":

> For a long time I had not visited the Municipal gallery. I went there a week ago, and was restored to many friends. I sat down, after a few minutes, overwhelmed with emotion. There were pictures painted by men, now dead, who were once my intimate friends ...

7

The Lash Goes On: Yeats' Epigrams

While there is not room in this study to discuss the plays or longer poems, we must squeeze in a brief acknowledgement of Yeats' skill as an epigrammatist. It is not a skill much valued these days, when the haiku is more to our taste, yet Geoffrey Grigson called it "an everlasting form"; and every memorable advertising jingle, limerick and epitaph is more or less epigrammatic. It is "a form of writing which makes a satiric, complimentary, or aphoristic observation with wit, extreme condensation, and, above all, brevity", better defined by its "ironic or gnomic" tone than by its verse form, though that is conventionally couplet or quatrain. So *The Princeton Encyclopaedia of Poetry and Poetics* tells us, but neglects to mention the essential ingredient: rhyme, and usually full rhyme.

It was not until the early 20th century that Yeats began to sharpen his satirical knives and write really effective epigrams, although there are plenty of short lyrical poems in earlier volumes and the 'Quatrains and Aphorisms' from *The Wanderings of Oisin and Other Poems* show the odd glint through the twilight. There are several characteristic types which he eventually mastered. The philosophical/occult epigrams include 'A Meditation in Time of War', 'Gratitude to the Unknown Instructors', 'A Needle's Eye' and 'There' (in a Blakean style later to be developed by Kathleen Raine). These tend to be short on wit, which a true epigram needs. Yeats was not good at humour, but a master of wit and for this we must look to the group of public/political verses I have chosen.

One of his most widely praised epigrams has a title half as long as the poem, but that is one of the traditions of the form: 'On hearing that the Students of our New University have joined the Agitation against Immoral Literature' is witty in the sense that Pope understood. The poet laughs in disbelief and mockery at young people behaving like sober citizens and "restraining reckless middle-age", the alliteration clinching the joke. The opening is an ear-catching guffaw, particularly if the 'h' is sounded in "where" so that it can spark with "here". It is a truly public utterance.

The *youth/truth* rhyme is always a favourite for Yeats; and middle-*age* naturally attracts *wage* just as the middle classes are attracted to a "greasy till". Other public statements are more gnomic ('On Those that Hated 'The Playboy of the Western World', 1907'), but in the epigrams from the late 1930s, no one can miss the point:

> Hurrah for revolution and more cannon shot;
> A beggar upon horseback lashes a beggar upon foot;
> Hurrah for revolution and cannon come again,
> The beggars have changed places but the lash goes on.

Here, in 'The Great Day', Yeats even risks half-rhyme, letting repetition and rhythm carry the satirical whip. 'Parnell', from the same period, does the same in just two lines: "Parnell came down the road, he said to a cheering man;/'Ireland shall get her freedom and you still break stone.'"

Literary/historical epigrams include a bite-size 'Dover Beach' in 'The Nineteenth Century and After'; the potted history of poetry from "Shakespearean fish" to "all those fish that lie gasping on the strand" in 'Three Movements' of three rhyming lines; the squib "Should H.G. Wells afflict you/Put whitewash in a pail;/Paint: 'Science – opium of the suburbs'/On some waste wall" and 'Swift's Epitaph'. Yeats showed in writing his own epitaph how he could find the *mot juste* for a headstone. For Swift, he lighted on "indignation", "lacerate" and came to rest on "liberty", in six potent trochaic trimeters, rhyming *ababcc*.

There is a range of personal/sexual epigrams, many commenting on poetry itself. The early 'To a Poet …' has a proud thrust in the last line "But was there ever a dog that praised his fleas?": what other poet could get away with that? More restrainedly, there is the revealing, untitled quatrain: "The friends that have it I do wrong/When ever I remake a song,/Should know what issue is at stake:/It is myself that I remake." Then there are curses, which need to be epigrammatic. We feel that Yeats really means it when he threatens to bring a curse down on any "who brings to light of day/The writings I have cast away!" He was, after all, a practising sorcerer. 'The Spur' is much quoted (note *rage/age*) for its candour about lust in an old man, and 'Politics' (a poem he was very proud of), though too long to be an epigram, uses all the epigrammatic devices, including wit, to achieve its effects. The key-shift from relaxed informality to a twinge of tense desire in the last two lines is quite brilliant.

Some of the epigrams depend on a clever conceit: 'The Balloon of the Mind', the unsettling 'A Stick of Incense', 'Statistics', 'Fragments'... There are several which hinge on the contrast between youth and age: 'The Coming of Wisdom with Time', an early poem, which extends its tree metaphor to another *truth/youth* rhyme; 'Youth and Age' (note *young/tongue*); and the rather poignant 'Spilt Milk' with its sad last simile, where we might detect some unconscious longing for the mother Yeats seldom wrote about. 'The Witch' hangs on a comparison, too ("Toil and grow rich,/What's that but to lie/ With a foul witch ..."): one that was even more shocking in the revision Yeats wanted to make, where the third line became "some stale bitch". Yeats is relating here a personal fairy story; but also a morality tale, reminding us that the beauty we all seek (not just those in love with Maud Gonne) is unavailable on this earth and certainly not to be found through material gain.

8

Sixty or More Winters: Yeats in Old Age

Having become a "sixty-year-old smiling public man" and survived a life-threatening illness the previous year, Yeats took stock, writing himself through his bitterness into some kind of acceptance. We see this process most nakedly in the sequence, 'The Tower' (composed 1925), which opens with a *cri de cœur* at the loss of youth and the inescapable humiliation that now awaits him as an old man. The tone is a mixture of sour resignation, Wordsworthian nostalgia ("No, not in boyhood …") defiance and grudging amusement. The image of a "battered kettle at the heel" (was he thinking of his critic, Tom Kettle?), with its tooth-grinding t-sounds, is a clownishly theatrical one, anticipating Beckett. The poem's extended middle section is another of Yeats' roll-calls, putting himself as new owner of Thoor Ballylee in the local historical context, summoning the folk poet Raftery and other Galway legends, including his own Hanrahan. He wishes to ask these characters a question, which he does nine stanzas later: "Did all old men and women, rich and poor,/Who trod upon these rocks or passed this door,/Whether in public or in secret rage/ As I do now against old age?" (pauses are necessary before "rage" and after "now" to catch the sense here). This leads him to further questions about love and how one may escape being haunted by "a woman won or a woman lost".

The third part of the triptych is calmer, accepting that he needs to prepare for leave-taking and consider those who will follow him (artists, rather than his children). There is a rather different cry from the heart – one of defiance, not pain, and the declaration of his creed ("That, being dead, we rise …") and his faith in the enduring power of art. Birds are used, as so often, for symbolic reinforcement: the "daws" (jackdaws) building a nest, the "bird's sleepy cry" at the close. The last twenty-three lines include a grimly affecting list of the possible ends of age. Yeats disproves his own disingenuous remark about "this sedentary trade" by following it with one of the most sinuous combinations of syntax and trimeter he ever composed. Its language anticipates 'Sailing to Byzantium', which would be written shortly after.

We tend to think of 'Sailing to Byzantium' as carved in stone, as one of those "monuments of unageing intellect" it describes. From its very opening, it resonates to a deep-flowing music: the words feel as if they could not follow any other pattern. Yet when Yeats came to read it for the BBC in 1937, he felt dissatisfied with the syntax and instead began:

> Old men should quit a country where the young
> In one another's arms; birds in the trees ...

In fact, the famous opening is masterly, from its short-breathed sigh of exasperation ("That is no country for old men.") to the subsequent sentence, which rides the line-breaks with an exuberance that belies any talk of decrepitude. The "country" described is not glossy-tourist-brochure Ireland, more a medieval or Chinese painting in which elements of everyday life overlap, indifferent to perspective: trees above seas next to lovers beside birds. Yeats uses his favourite *ottava rima* authoritatively, but not for narrative purposes (as Byron did): each of the four stanzas is a set piece, brought to a close by its final couplet, like the tinkling of a bell in an Orthodox service.

The Yeatsian music of repetition, echo and slightly muddy grammar, is ideal for the dream-like theme. Yet there is nothing dreamy about the rhythm or the diction, which is fresh and even colloquial, open to neologisms such as "perne" and "gyre". The poet desires to be gathered into "the artifice of eternity", to be forever the poet, forever a part of the Paterian music to which all art aspires. 'Sailing to Byzantium' is almost whimsical, but only in the way that a dream seems so when we wake from it: "gay" is a better word for the mood. How different, though, is the effect of this gaiety from that in other equivalent poems of escape, such as Stevenson's "I should like to rise and go ...", Flecker's 'Samarkand' or Yeats' own 'Innisfree'. Here we feel the pain of old age powering the poem, a lifetime's thought on art and the afterlife, and – most crucially – a refusal to give easy answers. Intensely memorable as it is, 'Sailing to Byzantium' plays hard to get, however many times we repeat it: following Yeats' earlier advice to lovers, it never gives "all the heart".

'Among Schoolchildren' (written in June 1926 and again in *ottava rima*) is twice the length of 'Sailing to Byzantium' and altogether more discursive, even occasionally running on between stanzas. A schoolroom could hardly be more of a contrast with Byzantium, but we do not stay long with the inspectorial mood ("to cut and sew, be neat in everything") and the "kind old nun" is soon forgotten in favour of "a Ledaean body", a memory of what (it is safe to assume) Maud Gonne has told him about her childhood. The sight of schoolgirls, mere "paddlers" compared to Leda, but who might look much as she did "at that age" brings out the wild old wicked man: "And thereupon my heart is driven wild:/She stands before me as a living child". Yeats is brought back to consciousness of his Senatorial role with a wry slapping down of his own vanity: "And I though never of Ledaean kind/Had pretty plumage once ..." He is suddenly aware of what he must look like to these children: he is a father himself now and knows how cruel children can be. His thoughts turn back to himself and his age. John Unterecker notes the "series of parallel trinities" in the poem: baby, child, scarecrow; lover, nun, mother; Plato, Aristotle, Pythagoras, etc. The image of the chestnut tree at the end is a means of uniting these strands as branches meet in a tree trunk. 'Among Schoolchildren' might have ended like 'The Municipal Gallery Revisited', with a resort to Beckettian silence; instead Yeats finds an adequate image to take the emotional strain. Rhetorical? Perhaps. And one could compare the very different, utterly undramatic use of the chestnut in Seamus Heaney's 'Clearances'. But no one would begrudge Yeats such a blazing finale.

On a very different scale, Yeats also wrote quiet, unaffected lyrics about growing old ('An Acre of Grass'), together with simple songs and ballads ('Song', 'The Three Hermits'), and even 'A Prayer for Old Age'. One of the finest of these miniatures is 'What Then?', which follows the course of a successful life through its stages, reminding us at each moment of success that worldly achievement does not amount to much: '*What then*?' *sang Plato's ghost*. '*What then*?', until finally, in sentiments not so very far from Frank Sinatra's 'My Way', punctured by that mocking ghost:

'The work is done,' grown old he thought,
'According to my boyish plan;
Let the fools rage, I swerved in nought,
Something to perfection brought';
But louder sang that ghost, 'What then?'

The paradoxical truth by which as a man grows older, he feels the "gaiety" of life more strongly (just as his youth was spent in melancholy thoughts of dying) is one that fascinated Yeats. It was part of his 'theory of gyres', his essentially antithetical view of human experience: "To me all things are made of the conflict of two states of consciousness," he wrote to Ethel Mannin near the end of his life, "beings or persons which die each other's life, live each other's death. This is true of life and death itself." We see this transcendent optimism in the face of bodily decrepitude at its highest pitch in 'Lapis Lazuli' and the defiant 'Under Ben Bulben', which will be discussed further in the next chapter. The triumphant final thoughts on age come in 'The Circus Animals' Desertion', composed between November of 1937 and September of 1938. Using *ottava rima* again and to quite different effect, Yeats constructs his three-part poem so that the first and last sections are single stanzas, meditating on old age and loss of creative power, while the three middle stanzas "enumerate old themes", running through some of the familiar names and topics that have preoccupied him. The effect is of curtains opening in Part I to present Part II's pageant, a passing carnival with Oisin, the Countess Cathleen, Cuchulain, only to have them close again for the epilogue (III). Originally, Yeats had planned an additional stanza, which would have upset the symmetry. A draft of it ("Even at the approach of the un-imagined night/Man has the refuge of his gaiety …" [spelt 'gaity']) was found on his desk when he died. Perhaps he thought to use it separately, just as the planned sixth stanza of 'Coole and Ballylee, 1931' became 'The Choice'.

Part I is Yeats at his most bare-boned, colloquial and throwaway ("six weeks or so", "the Lord knows what"), realising that all an aged poet has to write about is his heart, though the old "circus animals" and "stilted boys" and "burnished chariot" are waiting to perform again – by which he means the more exotic ideas, the lofty insights, the ambitious schemes. But the arena in which such poems are 'on show' seems tawdry and pointless to him now. No theme feels worth his while: he cannot bring himself to whip any more tricks out of the old faithfuls. The half-rhymes (*vain/man, chariot/what*) emphasise the lack of fulfilment, and the fact that this is a solitary stanza increases the sense of abandonment.

There is an upsurge of self-confidence as he brings to mind the characters who performed for him in the past, taking us on a brief autobiographical tour, everything funnelling back to Maud Gonne. So he implies that it was "vain gaiety, vain battle, vain repose" for him as for Oisin (he is thinking back to his first success, the long poem 'The Wanderings of Oisin'), because he too "starved for the bosom of his faery bride". "*The Countess Cathleen*" is recalled as representative of Yeats' dramatic ambitions and the Fenian "dream", which included an Irish National Theatre, but she was, of course, modelled on Maud Gonne. Finally, Cuchulain appears, who "fought the ungovernable sea", and although Yeats himself withstood many tidal forces, the use of that adjective "ungovernable" suggests that he is thinking of his own role in government. Public responsibilities are, he implies (and Prospero might have agreed) like those of the stage producer: "when all is said/It was the dream itself enchanted me ... Players and painted stage took all my love,/And not those things that they were emblems of." Naturally, the wonderful thing about these lines is that they can be applied to so many situations in Yeats' life or in our own.

The celebrated final stanza with its repeated use of "old" harks back to an idea in *A Vision*, where (as quoted by Roy Foster) he had associated the Muse with "women who creep out at night and give themselves to unknown sailors". Now he must look for inspiration in "that raving slut/Who keeps the till" – perhaps, humiliatingly, that same greasy till featured in 'September 1913'? The poet of twilight and the "heaven's embroidered cloths" and "the bee-loud glade" has no dreams left, only "a mound of refuse or the sweepings of a street": more than a token gesture to T.S. Eliot and his "smell of steaks in passageways" and signifying something considerably deeper for his personal aesthetic:

> Now that my ladder's gone,
> I must lie down where all the ladders start,
> In the foul rag-and-bone shop of the heart.

As William H. Pritchard put it: “has there ever been a more sensational promise to lie down?”

9

This Sedentary Trade: Yeats and the Art of Poetry

Poets naturally write about the business of writing, but for Yeats it became one of his major themes. This chapter will focus on poems from over 45 years in which he explores the poet's responsibilities. He was always intensely aware of his Anglo-Irish heritage, that he not only had to live up to major figures such as Spenser (with all the political difficulties that name implies) but "be counted one/With Davis, Mangan, Ferguson", iconic figures of the Irish literary revival. At Thoor Ballylee, he was as conscious of the legendary blind local bard Eoghan O'Rahilly as he was of Homer. He remained alert to the work of international figures such as Joyce, without forsaking writers who would never be widely known beyond Ireland. And he speaks freely (in 'Under Ben Bulben' and 'The Tower') to the poets of "coming days", advising them to learn their trade.

Once his poetic reputation was established, there was the inevitable backlash and Yeats found himself having to defend his work. The last poem in *The Rose*, 'To Ireland in the Coming Times' (originally published in 1892 with *The Countess Cathleen* – and always italicized) is part of this defence as well as a declaration of artistic ambition. Yeats is responding to members of the Rhymers' Club, his old "companions of the Cheshire Cheese", who had accused him of obscurity; and to Maud Gonne and John O'Leary who thought his work was not sufficiently Fenian. This particular poem should have satisfied them since, although it invokes the ultimate power of the mystical Rose and "things discovered in the deep", it does so with perfect clarity and proclaims the artist as shaper of events. As Stephen Coote puts it: "by staring deep into his heart and the *anima mundi* he has brought forth the great images that must by their very nature inspire men to action." Yeats shows his early mastery in the use of repetition and refrain (the elemental creatures which "*go/About my table to and fro*") and his Shakespearean pithiness. Prospero's epilogue comes to mind, or the spell-like iambic tetrameters of Hecate in *Macbeth*. This choice of metre in itself asserts Yeats' loyalty to ceremonial magic. But 'To Ireland in the Coming Times' has the forward momentum of a ballad too, and has some perceptive things to say about art's place in the world.

'Adam's Curse', written 10 years later, is a complete contrast. It is a relaxed, meditative, nostalgic poem which contains some of Yeats' most illuminating comments on what he called (in 'The Tower') "this sedentary trade". Maud Gonne recalled the occasion that inspired the poem, a conversation she and her sister had with Willy in which "Kathleen remarked that it was hard work being beautiful". The following day he again begged Maud to put an end to his unhappiness; but she answered shrewdly: "you make beautiful poetry out of what you call your unhappiness ... The world should thank me for not marrying you." The first section of 'Adam's Curse' contains the insights on the poet's role: how art must conceal art and "seem a moment's thought", even though a line may take hours; how writing poetry is even harder work than scrubbing floors or breaking stone (a theory we can safely assume Yeats did not put to the test); how the poet will always be considered an "idler" by the world ("bankers, schoolmasters and clergymen"). The conversation moves from the sacrifices made for poetry to those (taken from Kathleen's remark) made for beauty and the mention of love eventually silences all three of them. Of course, the poem itself goes on 'speaking' for another 10 lines, which is perhaps Yeats' way of having the last word.

The 'labour' of writing is a favourite topic in his middle period poems. In the lines from 1908 that begin "All things can tempt me from this craft of verse ..." poetry is "accustomed toil", and the 20th-century Yeats is only too aware that what he looks for in the finished work is now very different. He used to aspire to something heroic, declaimed as if "he had a sword upstairs" (ironically, Sato's sword will come to mean something much loftier), but now feels he is in a different poetic element, where he can only be "colder and dumber and deafer than a fish". He was very involved with "plays/ That have to be set up in fifty ways", and 'The Fascination of What's

Difficult' (1909), with its lament for the loss of spontaneity and joy, reflects this commitment to the ruthless needs of the theatre as much as his feelings about stylistic developments. Inspiration is symbolised as an Olympian winged horse who is forced to "Shiver under the lash" and drag "road metal". At this point, there is no appeal to Yeats in such rag-and-bone-shop earthiness. All he wants is to "find the stable and pull out the bolt": i.e. find the opportunity to release his best poetry.

By 1912, however, he will be expressing the wish to escape "embroideries" and "mythologies", finding "more enterprise/In walking naked". The 10 short lines of 'A Coat', which first appeared at the very end of *Responsibilities*, mark the shift in Yeats' poetic style which dominates that collection. He addresses his own "song" and tells it that the world can interpret his dreams however it wishes: he will go on writing about the (sometimes unpalatable) realities of waking life. At the opening of *Responsibilities* stands a curious experiment, 'The Grey Rock', which mingles an address to those same (now dead) "companions" of the Rhymers' Club "with whom I learned my trade" and a legend of the Irish gods in which "the sacred stuff" brewed by Goban has something in common with the Norse gods' mead of poetic inspiration. The poem asks how much priority friends, country or beloved should each be given. It adapts and embroiders a fairy tale about Aoibhell (Aoife), who offered Dubhlaing O'Hartagan two hundred years in her company on the condition that he abandoned his friend, the King of Ireland's son. He refused, claiming (Aoife tells us) "his country's need was most,/I'd saved his life, yet for the sake/Of a new friend he has turned a ghost ..." Yeats wonders whether the ghosts of *his* friends, Lionel Johnson and Ernest Dowson, might now actually know that he was right to be so preoccupied with the gods ("Maybe your images have stood ... Before that roomful") but also tells us what he admired in their work.

The poet as misunderstood outsider tiptoes through Yeats' work. In 'The Scholars', he (and it is always "he", an issue Eavan Boland has made one of her own central themes as a poet) is tossing on his bed while "old, learned, respectable bald heads/Edit and annotate" his lines. Yeats, who never completed a university course himself, remarks delightfully: "Lord, what would they say/Did their Catullus walk that way?", the answer being, they would probably be as shocked as if they met Eminem or Sid Vicious. But Yeats would probably have found Catullus hard going, too. He was fairly selective about humanity, as suggested in 'The Fisherman' (composed June 1914) where he writes of "the living men that I hate,/The dead men that I loved,/The craven man in his seat,/The insolent unreproved ..." and so on. At the heart of this fine poem stands the "freckled man who goes/To a grey place on a hill/In grey Connamara clothes/At dawn to cast his flies". This visionary figure is not exactly Yeats' ideal reader, but the one for whom he imagines his poems to be written, the face of "What I had hoped 'twould be/To write for my own race". Eavan Boland has written very persuasively in *Object Lessons* about the muse and other "simplifications of women" in Irish poetry, but here for once is a man fulfilling that inspirational role. The fisherman is a personification of the new style Yeats is hoping to perfect, "wise and simple...Climbing up to a place/Where stone is dark under froth". The vision moves him to cry out in the last few iambic tetrameters, with a metrical inversion on the word "poem", which then ricochets off "passionate" in the next line:

> ' ... Before I am old
> I shall have written him one
> Poem maybe as cold
> And passionate as the dawn.'

Who is better than W.B. Yeats at ending a poem?

As politics and the occult become uppermost in Yeats' thoughts, there are fewer poems about the ideology of writing until we reach his late period. That is not to say that 'being a poet' is any less important to him: indeed, it is a measure of how he views his place in the world that at the end of the First World War he is carving his own lines on his own tower to mark its restoration: "And may these characters remain/When all is ruin once again." By the time he is writing his last poems, it is taken for granted that he is The Poet, almost a figure of myth himself: certainly, he could be forgiven for feeling that way, so desperate were his fans to worship him, so freely were the honours lavished on him. In 'The Choice' (1931), perhaps weary of the public role, he implies that a poet must choose "perfection of the life or of the work". But by this time he is less interested in the poet's task than in the broader significance of the artist in society.

'Lapis Lazuli' was completed in July 1936 and is one of his most enduring poems. Its dedicatee, Harry Clifton, had given him a medallion of the blue and gold-flecked stone (most famously used in the Tutankhamun treasures) and the image of the Chinese man and his servant becomes the "two Chinamen, behind them a third" of the poem's final section. 'Lapis Lazuli' opens provocatively, with anger, exasperation and a good deal of colloquial language in its bitter sarcasm – "For everybody knows or else should know/That if nothing drastic is done ..." The tone of 'September 1913' is audible here. This time Yeats is mocking those who fret and fuss about how bad things are, who go around saying something ought to be done, and who moan about poets who don't contribute. Although he mentions "hysterical women", in some respects this is aimed at the 1930s poets (including the latest Irish voice: Louis MacNeice) who were openly and partisanly political in their writings, who believed that poets should see that something "drastic is done" – although Auden, for one, would eventually acknowledge in his elegy to Yeats that "poetry makes nothing happen". Yeats knows tragedy when he sees it and this is not it, he says: it's no good pulling on the tragic buskin and strutting around like Hamlet if you haven't realised the essential truth that "Hamlet and Lear are gay;/Gaiety transfiguring all that dread."

'Lapis Lazuli' is composed in Yeats' late, Modernist manner, using what John Unterecker (in his very detailed analysis) describes as "planes which – fitted together by the reader – form a coherent object". The verse shows Yeats at his most succinct: "All men have aimed at, found and lost", he tells us, without saying what they aimed at. The point is that it scarcely matters, whether they are revolutionary sculptors (like Callimachus) or anonymous "Chinamen", the end is "Black out". We are back with Prospero again and the vision that vanishes and leaves not a rack behind. The shifts of key are miraculous, gradually moving closer and closer to the 'home key' of the lapis lazuli image. "On their own feet they came ...", the third section begins. Who are "they" and where have they come to? Is Yeats thinking of the refugees that the 1930s poets were writing about? It is a sudden cinematic shift or one of those grinding juxtapositions of keys from a symphony by Carl Nielsen (born in the same year as Yeats). By the end of the section we see the connection: this is a plea for individuation ("On their own feet ..."), for moving forward, not shaking our heads sadly over "King Billy"; and it is a smile in the face of the inevitable: "All things fall and are built again/And those that build them again are gay."

Many commentators have noted the similarities between Yeats' use of the carving on the medallion and Keats' in 'On a Grecian Urn' (though we should not forget *Ille*'s revealing vision of Keats as "a schoolboy ... With face and nose pressed to a sweet-shop window" in 'Ego Dominus Tuus'). The way in which Yeats draws us in to the detail, zooming to a close-up on "Every discolouration of the stone,/ Every accidental crack or dent", in elevated language which is a far cry from the gossipy opening, is unsurpassed in his work. In 'Sailing to Byzantium' the poet tells us how he will "set upon a golden bough", but never takes us with him: here, we are led into the scene, joining poet and Chinese sages. The eyes are mentioned three times, once for each "Chinaman". "One asks for mournful melodies" with a trochee and a touch of alliteration. "Accomplished" speaks of culture and time-honed skills. "Wrinkles" tell us that the poet has climbed too high to be bothered with his "pretty plumage". It is not only those "glittering eyes" that make us feel like the wedding guest being grasped by the Ancient Mariner.

'Long-legged Fly' was written between November 1937 and April 1938 (it was completed at Steyning, Sussex), and while it does not speak directly about the art of the poet, the refrain suggests a continual return to the poetic springs and might even remind us of 'The Fisherman': "*Like a long-legged fly upon the stream/His mind moves upon silence*." Reading this poem, one feels part of some Masonic geometry linking Caesar and Helen and 'Michael Angelo'. The fate of civilisations hangs on trivial details; epic histories are born out of "nothing" or "a tinker shuffle"; art quietly defies its most puritanical opponents; contact with the sources of true understanding is fleeting and almost imperceptible, like that fly on the water.

'Long-legged Fly' is Yeats' last great lyric poem. The 'suite' or short sequence, 'Under Ben Bulben', was completed on 4th September 1938 only five months before his death: it is an elegy to himself and a tribute to poetry's place in history. It was written at a time when he was drawn to ideas on eugenics, something which gives the poem a disturbing undertow. In six parts, it opens with characteristic occult and historical allusions: Alexandria's Lake Mareotis (home of Monastic learning) and the Witch of Atlas (who could summon the dead, though she owes more to Shelley than the Bible). The metre echoes 'To Ireland in the Coming Times', written nearly half a century earlier, but with much greater use of trochaics:

> *Swear* by what the Sages spoke
> *Round* the Mareotic Lake
> *That* the Witch of Atlas knew,
> *Spoke* and set the cocks a-crow …

There is a curious ambiguity in Yeats' use of "that" as determiner or pronoun (Swear that the witch in fact knew? Swear that which she knew?) here and further on: "That pale, long-visaged company/That air in immortality …" Even without the much-reproduced substitution of 'an' for 'in', it is, in fact, a clumsy stanza, something indicative of a man who is (as Brenda Maddox says) "vacillating to the end" but who is trying to sound dogmatic. The 'Creed' (Yeats' original title for the poem) appears in Part II, with its proclamation of faith in life's continuation: "A brief parting from those dear/Is the worst man has to fear." Part III develops notions from Rilke, whose influence is strong throughout, that "a man's death is born with him … his nature is completed by his final union with it" and parodies the language of the Munich agreement by quoting the 19th-century nationalist John Mitchel's "Send war in our time, O Lord", Yeats suggesting that at 'predestined moments' one can be elevated to a level of superhuman insight from which one can "accomplish fate".

In Parts IV and V Yeats turns to the position of the artist. His ideas owe much to the theory of gyres which emerged from *A Vision* and where it is more fully explained. Essentially, he imagines contrary cone-shaped forces ever expanding and contracting within each other through the cycles of history and through any individual life, as in the following illustration:

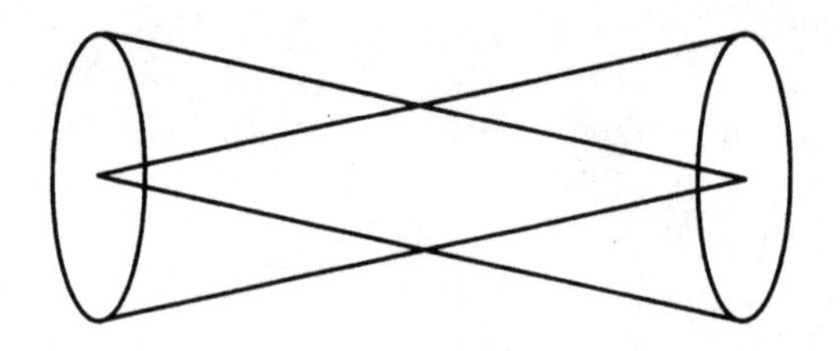

Yeats wrote of 'Under Ben Bulben': "it gets into narrow space what I think about the break between ancient and modern art" and Part IV is a call to modern artists to draw on their "great forefathers", to make their lines (in a gyre-like geometry) lead right back to Greece and Egypt and to conjure 'heavens' as the 15th-century Italian artists and later the English visionaries could. Ironically, there is once again a grammatical haziness in the line "Forms a stark Egyptian thought", where we are unclear at first what is noun and what is verb.

Part V looks to the future and appeals to "Irish poets" to be craftsmen and to "Sing whatever is well made". It is, Brenda Maddox reminds us, "an order that...continues to ring, perhaps too loudly, in the ears of every Irish poet since Yeats". There is ill-concealed bitterness under the rather forced gaiety of the trochaic tetrameter: "Irish … Sing … Scorn …" Although the language owes something to the poet's reading about eugenics ("All out of shape from top to toe … Base-born products of base beds") he is really more concerned with style than race, thinking of extreme modernists and sloppy political versifiers as much as the detested middle classes. It is hard, though, to imagine what kind of poems he was recommending young writers to produce on the basis of his list of suitable themes: "Hard-riding country gentlemen,/The holiness of monks, and after/Porter-drinkers' randy laughter … "

The final part of 'Under Ben Bulben' is well known, as it contains the epitaph he composed for himself. Less well known is that one version of it ran:

> Draw rein, draw breath!
> Cast a cold eye
> On life, on death.
> Huntsman, pass by!

The three lines as we know them have a more haiku-like impact. "Horseman" is certainly more universal but also more sinister than "Huntsman". Nevertheless, those missing four words have considerable power. It is significant that in the preliminary rhymes, after the assertive trochee and the Drumcliff-drum-beat of b's, and before the mild discord of the half rhyme (*head/laid*), the poet now speaks of himself in the third person:

> Under bare Ben Bulben's head
> In Drumcliff churchyard Yeats is laid …

He has already joined the pantheon and "his command" comes like that of a god.

10

A Stone to Trouble the Living Stream: The Influence of Yeats

At his death, in 1939, Yeats was one of the most widely read poets in the English-speaking world. Even as dissimilar a writer as W.H. Auden was moved to compose an acclaimed elegy, reporting on "the death of the poet" as if it were an international crisis: "The provinces of his body revolted,/The squares of his mind were empty,/Silence invaded the suburbs,/The current of his feeling failed: he became his admirers." Another member of the 1930s group, Louis MacNeice, might have felt that he was expected to take up the mantle, and indeed he wrote a fine book about his countryman (and another on astrology, which Yeats would have appreciated). But MacNeice always had a distinctive voice of his own and would, in fact, offer many younger Irish poets – Derek Mahon, for one – a way of skirting round "the Grey Rock" of WBY. In general, however, the "coming" Irish poets would have to measure up to his example either by defying him or by trying to equal him. The exhortation in 'Under Ben Bulben' to "learn your trade" could not simply be forgotten.

Robert Garratt, in *Modern Irish Poetry*, (1986), has remarked that "the demythologising of the Yeatsian poetic tradition has become a regular and important act for almost every Irish poet" – and indeed Yeats left plenty of ammunition for such attacks. The sheer humourless obscurity of some of the poetry, the airy nothingness of the fairy verse and what is routinely called the 'mumbo jumbo' of his occult obsessions; the haughtiness of tone, the fondness for divisive, aristocratic values, the snobbishness; the simplification of women to goddesses or lovers; the nepotism and cliquiness in his literary judgements; the accusations of fascism ... All this has been packed into many a hefty critical cannon and let roar at the sacred image. But any psychoanalyst will explain how the patient attacks the person he or she is in love with, and the assaults either from within Ireland or beyond have hardly affected Yeats' critical standing or, more importantly, his popular following. Brenda Maddox has been one of the few to use the most effective weapon of all – affectionate laughter. And Auden's word "silly" is still one of the best for some of Yeats' antics. Those who have not been able to smile have, like Philip Larkin, turned away, found comfort in realism or gloomy irony. Yes, there is some necessary debunking to be done in reading Yeats and disbelief has to be willingly suspended. Nor has the ghost of fascist sympathies been laid: but it never manifests itself in the poetry as, say, Eliot's anti-Semitism does.

Irish poets who felt uncomfortable under the shadow of Ben Bulben could follow Louis MacNeice or Patrick Kavanagh away from what Bernard O'Donoghue calls the "Celtic high ground". But post-war writers as diverse as Austin Clarke, John Montague and Thomas Kinsella are touched by it. When Seamus Heaney emerged with *Death of a Naturalist* in 1966 it was inevitable that he would be labelled "the greatest Irish poet since Yeats", even though what was striking about his work was how he seemed to have freed himself from the 'presence'. Only in later writings would Heaney begin to use those resources, stirred by the Troubles as his predecessor was by the Easter Rising, using the local myths, making a Coole Park of Toome or Mossbawn, even edging towards some of the same literary ground in his translations of Greek drama. For emerging women poets of the following decades in Ireland, there were different challenges, involving the 'Muse' and certain archetypal female figures. Eavan Boland finds a cache of poetic material entirely untouched by Yeats in the everyday life of a suburban Irishwoman. In 'The Oral Tradition' or her sequence 'Outside History' she explores areas that would have bewildered him. And yet she knows that there is something in her voice that could not have sounded without the master's key-note. Brendan Kennelly is tuning to it when he writes of his "man made of rain": so is Paul Durcan when he pleases a crowd with a chanted refrain; and Paul Muldoon as he disappears into the semantic twilight. Irish poets of the twenty-first century are beginning to find that they can return to that home key, to remind themselves where they left Yeats and turn over his bones without fear of raising troublesome spirits: encouraged, perhaps, by a renewed debate as to whether his body was ever actually 'laid to rest' in Drumcliff Churchyard at all.

English, Welsh and Scottish poets of the immediate post-Second World War period were steeped in Yeatsian rhetoric, too: George Barker, Vernon Watkins, Edwin Muir … There are surprising cases, such as Larkin, particularly in his early collection, *The North Ship*, but for all his Hardyesque earthiness, the Yeatsian mysteries slip through in the imagery at the end of 'The Whitsun Weddings' and 'High Windows'. Larkin's Oxford anthology of contemporary verse was, incidentally, the successor to Yeats': both were utterly idiosyncratic. One might have expected the 'Movement' poets of the 1950s to shake Yeats off for good, but he is there in the pentameters of Elizabeth Jennings, for example, as much as in the incantations of that great symbolist survivor, Kathleen Raine. With the revival of interest in Blake and revolution and free love and the occult in the 1960s, it became apparent that he was not going to go away. Ted Hughes, born the year that Yeats rejected the idea of becoming Laureate, was much indebted to the mage and visionary; Sylvia Plath was equally fascinated. In late 1962, she instinctively knew that she had found "*the* street and *the* house" to rent when she saw the blue plaque on the wall. In one of her last letters she asked for the Irish poet, Richard Murphy, to be told where she was living, saying that Yeats' name on the building was "a real inspiration" to her writing. It was at 23 Fitzroy Road that she killed herself.

While the Hughes/Plath mythology has been ramifying with the help of *Birthday Letters*, less well known English poets have continued to grapple with Yeatsian forces. Even though T.S. Eliot thought in 1940 that his idiom would prove "too different for there to be any danger of imitation" (and then gave him a walk-on part in 'Little Gidding'!) we find traces of it from Peter Redgrove to Peter Scupham, from Penelope Shuttle to Pauline Stainer, from Jack Clemo to Geoffrey Hill. Those who could resist his influence might turn instead to parody, as in William Scammell's wonderful Wimbledon spin on 'Sailing to Byzantium': "A backhand slice is but a paltry shot …" Those who could not, might see themselves swallowed by the maw of Yeatsian rhetoric. In America, Theodore Roethke quite lost his way because of the influence: "I take this cadence from a man named Yeats ..." he wrote in 'Four for Sir John Davies'. But he took more than the cadence – one of the 'Four' begins: "Incomprehensible gaiety and dread/Attended what we did ..." Robert Lowell and John Berryman, too, found him hard to shake off, though free verse helped the former and 'Dream Songs' the latter. Others gently incorporated Yeats into their universe, Archibald MacLeish defiantly staking out an American brand of Yeatsian public verse; and, later, James Merrill giving 'WBY' a speaking part in his trilogy *The Changing Light at Sandover* (1983), the product, appropriately, of epic Ouija board sessions (the voices of 'spirits' are all upper case):

> O SHINING AUDIENCE, IF AN OLD MAN'S SPEECH
> STIFF FROM LONG SILENCE CAN NO LONGER STRETCH
> TO THAT TOP SHELF OF RIGHTFUL BARD'S APPAREL
> FOR WYSTAN AUDEN & JAMES MEREL
> WHO HAVE REFASHIONED US BY FASHIONING THIS,
> MAY THE YOUNG SINGER HEARD ABOVE
> THE SPINNING GYRES OF HER TRUE LOVE
> CLOAK THEM IN HEAVEN'S AIRLOOM HARMONIES.

To which 'Nature' responds: "NOT RUSTY AFTER ALL, GOOD YEATS." Merrill (or his 'control') captures Yeats' poor spelling as well as he does his stanza form.

Elsewhere, the examples of Yeats' international influence are plentiful: poets have responded to a voice that could so lyrically express the soul of a people. At least three winners of the Nobel Prize for Literature seem indebted to him: Derek Walcott (St Lucia) and Wole Soyinka (Nigeria), particularly in their verse drama, but also for the lyric voice; and the Russian, Joseph Brodsky, whose translators find themselves turning to Ireland for an adequate music. But there are quieter voices that echo to his strains: James Baxter from New Zealand, for example, and the Australian, Gwen Harwood. Even now, books of poetry are published for which the only adjective a reviewer can find is 'Yeatsian'. Beyond the world of literature, Yeats has been widely set to music, ranging from the sweet folk simplicity of Christy Moore's 'Song of Wandering Aengus' to Michael Tippett's richly complex 'Byzantium'. But the ultimate prize for any poet is to become a part of everyday language: "no country for old men", "know the dancer from the dance", "things fall apart", "rag-and-bone shop of the heart", "I will arise and go now", "my glory was I had such friends", "a terrible beauty", "the innocent and the beautiful", "the last romantics", "cast a cold eye on life, on death" ... When Colonel Tim Collins addressed his troops in Iraq before battle, Yeats was there telling them to "tread lightly". Quoting or misquoting, we speak Yeats as we speak Shakespeare, Wordsworth, Cowper, Tennyson – without even knowing we do so. Perhaps, then, it is not surprising that in 2002 the distinguished critic Ian Hamilton felt he could confidently exclude W.B. Yeats from his "lives of 20th-century poets", *Against Oblivion.* For Yeats (like Hardy, Eliot and Auden), he was sure that "oblivion presents no threat".

Further Reading

and books referred to in the text

Books by W.B. Yeats

The Poems, ed. R.J. Finneran (Macmillan, 1983)
The Poems, ed. Daniel Albright (Dent, 1994)
Poems: a New Selection, ed. A. Norman Jeffares (Macmillan, 1984)
Poems selected by Seamus Heaney (Faber, 2000)
Collected Plays, (Macmillan, 1953)
Letters, selection, ed. Allen Wade (Hart-Davis, 1954)
Autobiographies (Macmillan, 1955)
Essays and Introductions (Macmillan, 1961)
Selected Criticism, ed. Jeffares (Pan, 1976)
A Vision (Macmillan, 1962)
Oxford Book of Modern Verse (Clarendon Press, 1936)
Audiobook NA 226412 (Naxos, 2004): readings and life, ed. Kavanagh

Biographies, Critical Studies, Essays

Eavan Boland, *Object Lessons* (Vintage, 1996)
Stephen Coote, *W.B.Yeats: A Life* (Hodder and Stoughton, 1997)
Raymond Cowell, *W.B. Yeats (Literature in Perspective)* (Evans, 1969)
T.S. Eliot, *On Poetry and Poets* (Faber, 1957)
R.F. Foster, *W.B. Yeats: A Life. I. The Apprentice Mage* (OUP, 1997)
II. The Arch-Poet (OUP, 2003)
Robert F. Garratt, *Modern Irish Poetry* (University of California, 1986)
Seamus Heaney, *Finders Keepers* (Faber, 2002)
T.R. Henn, *The Lonely Tower* (Methuen, 1950)
Joseph Hone, *W.B. Yeats* (Macmillan, 1942)

Randall Jarrell, *Kipling, Auden & Co.* (Carcanet, 1986)
A. Norman Jeffares, *W.B. Yeats: a New Biography* (Hutchinson, 1988)
F.R. Leavis, *New Bearings in English Poetry* (Penguin, 1972)
Louis MacNeice, *The Poetry of W.B. Yeats* (Faber, 1967)
Brenda Maddox, *George's Ghosts* (Picador, 1999)
Edward Malins and John Purkis, *A Preface to Yeats* (Longman, 1994)
William H. Pritchard, *Lives of the Modern Poets* (Faber, 1980)
C.H. Sisson, *English Poetry 1900-1950* (Carcanet, 1981)
C.K. Stead, *Pound, Yeats, Eliot and the Modernist Movement* (Macmillan, 1986)
John Unterecker, *A Reader's Guide to W.B. Yeats* (Thames and Hudson, 1959)

GREENWICH EXCHANGE BOOKS

LITERARY SERIES

The Greenwich Exchange Literary Series is a collection of critical essays of major or contemporary serious writers in English and selected European languages. The series is for the student, the teacher and 'common readers' and is an ideal resource for libraries. The *Times Educational Supplement* praised these books, saying, "The style of [this series] has a pressure of meaning behind it. Readers should learn from that ... If art is about selection, perception and taste, then this is it."

(ISBN prefix 1-871551- applies)
All books are paperbacks unless otherwise stated

The series includes:
W.H. Auden by Stephen Wade (36-6)
Honoré de Balzac by Wendy Mercer (48-X)
William Blake by Peter Davies (27-7)
The Brontës by Peter Davies (24-2)
Robert Browning by John Lucas (59-5)
Byron by Andrew Keanie (83-9)
Samuel Taylor Coleridge by Andrew Keanie (64-1)
Joseph Conrad by Martin Seymour-Smith (18-8)
William Cowper by Michael Thorn (25-0)
Charles Dickens by Robert Giddings (26-9)
Emily Dickinson by Marnie Pomeroy (68-4)
John Donne by Sean Haldane (23-4)
Ford Madox Ford by Anthony Fowles (63-3)
The Stagecraft of Brian Friel by David Grant (74-9)
Robert Frost by Warren Hope (70-6)
Thomas Hardy by Sean Haldane (33-1)
Seamus Heaney by Warren Hope (37-4)
Joseph Heller by Anthony Fowles (84-6)
Gerard Manley Hopkins by Sean Sheehan (77-3)
James Joyce by Michael Murphy (73-0)
Laughter in the Dark – The Plays of Joe Orton by Arthur Burke (56-0)
Philip Larkin by Warren Hope (35-8)
Poets of the First World War by John Greening (79-X)
Philip Roth by Paul McDonald (72-2)
Shakespeare's *Macbeth* by Matt Simpson (69-2)
Shakespeare's *Othello* by Matt Simpson (71-4)

Shakespeare's *The Tempest* by Matt Simpson (75-7)
Shakespeare's *Twelfth Night* by Matt Simpson (86-2)
Shakespeare's Non-Dramatic Poetry by Martin Seymour-Smith (22-6)
Shakespeare's Sonnets by Martin Seymour-Smith (38-2)
Shakespeare's *The Winter's Tale* by John Lucas (80-3)
Tobias Smollett by Robert Giddings (21-8)
Dylan Thomas by Peter Davies (78-1)
Alfred, Lord Tennyson by Michael Thorn (20-X)
William Wordsworth by Andrew Keanie (57-9)
W.B. Yeats by John Greening (34-X)

LITERATURE & BIOGRAPHY

Matthew Arnold and 'Thyrsis' *by Patrick Carill Connolly*
Matthew Arnold (1822-1888) was a leading poet, intellect and aesthete of the Victorian epoch. He is now best known for his strictures as a literary and cultural critic, and educationist. After a long period of neglect, his views have come in for a re-evaluation. Arnold's poetry remains less well known, yet his poems and his understanding of poetry, which defied the conventions of his time, were central to his achievement.
The author traces Arnold's intellectual and poetic development, showing how his poetry gathers its meanings from a lifetime's study of European literature and philosophy. Connolly's unique exegesis of 'Thyrsis' draws upon a wide-ranging analysis of the pastoral and its associated myths in both classical and native cultures. This study shows lucidly and in detail how Arnold encouraged the intense reflection of the mind on the subject placed before it, believing in " ... the all importance of the choice of the subject, the necessity of accurate observation; and subordinate character of expression."
Patrick Carill Connolly gained his English degree at Reading University and taught English literature abroad for a number of years before returning to Britain. He is now a civil servant living in London.
2004 • 180 pages • ISBN 1-871551-61-7

The Author, the Book and the Reader *by Robert Giddings*
This collection of essays analyses the effects of changing technology and the attendant commercial pressures on literary styles and subject matter. Authors covered include Charles Dickens, Tobias Smollett, Mark Twain, Dr Johnson and John le Carré.
1991 • 220 pages • illustrated • ISBN 1-871551-01-3

Aleister Crowley and the Cult of Pan *by Paul Newman*
Few more nightmarish figures stalk English literature than Aleister Crowley (1875-1947), poet, magician, mountaineer and agent provocateur. In this groundbreaking study, Paul Newman dives into the occult mire of Crowley's works and fishes out gems and grotesqueries that are by turns ethereal, sublime, pornographic and horrifying. Like Oscar Wilde before him, Crowley stood in "symbolic relationship to his age" and to contemporaries like Rupert Brooke, G.K. Chesterton and the Portuguese modernist, Fernando Pessoa. An influential exponent of the cult of the Great God Pan, his essentially 'pagan' outlook was shared by major European writers as well as English novelists like E.M. Forster, D.H. Lawrence and Arthur Machen.
Paul Newman lives in Cornwall. Editor of the literary magazine *Abraxas*, he has written over ten books.
2004 • 222 pages • ISBN 1-871551-66-8

John Dryden *by Anthony Fowles*
Of all the poets of the Augustan age, John Dryden was the most worldly. Anthony Fowles traces Dryden's evolution from 'wordsmith' to major poet. This critical study shows a poet of vigour and technical panache whose art was forged in the heat and battle of a turbulent polemical and pamphleteering age. Although Dryden's status as a literary critic has long been established, Fowles draws attention to his neglected achievements as a translator of poetry. He deals also with the less well-known aspects of Dryden's work – his plays and occasional pieces.
Born in London and educated at the Universities of Oxford and Southern California, Anthony Fowles began his career in film-making before becoming an author of film and television scripts and more than twenty books. Readers will welcome the many contemporary references to novels and film with which Fowles illuminates the life and work of this decisively influential English poetic voice.
2003 • 292 pages • ISBN 1-871551-58-7

The Good That We Do *by John Lucas*
John Lucas' book blends fiction, biography and social history in order to tell the story of his grandfather, Horace Kelly. Headteacher of a succession of elementary schools in impoverished areas of London, 'Hod' Kelly was also a keen cricketer, a devotee of the music hall, and included among his friends the great trade union leader Ernest Bevin. In telling the story of his life, Lucas has provided a fascinating range of insights into the lives of ordinary Londoners from the First World War until the outbreak of the Second World War. Threaded throughout is an account of such people's

hunger for education, and of the different ways government, church and educational officialdom ministered to that hunger. *The Good That We Do* is both a study of one man and of a period when England changed, drastically and forever.
John Lucas is Professor Emeritus of the Universities of Loughborough and Nottingham Trent. He is the author of numerous works of a critical and scholarly nature and has published seven collections of poetry.
2001 • 214 pages • ISBN 1-871551-54-4

In Pursuit of Lewis Carroll *by Raphael Shaberman*
Sherlock Holmes and the author uncover new evidence in their investigations into the mysterious life and writing of Lewis Carroll. They examine published works by Carroll that have been overlooked by previous commentators. A newly-discovered poem, almost certainly by Carroll, is published here.
Amongst many aspects of Carroll's highly complex personality, this book explores his relationship with his parents, numerous child friends, and the formidable Mrs Liddell, mother of the immortal Alice. Raphael Shaberman was a founder member of the Lewis Carroll Society and a teacher of autistic children.
1994 • 118 pages • illustrated • ISBN 1-871551-13-7

Liar! Liar!: Jack Kerouac – Novelist *by R.J. Ellis*
The fullest study of Jack Kerouac's fiction to date. It is the first book to devote an individual chapter to every one of his novels. *On the Road*, *Visions of Cody* and *The Subterraneans* are reread in-depth, in a new and exciting way. *Visions of Gerard* and *Doctor Sax* are also strikingly reinterpreted, as are other daringly innovative writings, like 'The Railroad Earth' and his "try at a spontaneous *Finnegans Wake*" – *Old Angel Midnight.* Neglected writings, such as *Tristessa* and *Big Sur*, are also analysed, alongside better-known novels such as *Dharma Bums* and *Desolation Angels.*
R.J. Ellis is Senior Lecturer in English at Nottingham Trent University.
1999 • 294 pages • ISBN 1-871551-53-6

Musical Offering *by Yolanthe Leigh*
In a series of vivid sketches, anecdotes and reflections, Yolanthe Leigh tells the story of her growing up in the Poland of the 1930s and the Second World War. These are poignant episodes of a child's first encounters with both the enchantments and the cruelties of the world; and from a later time, stark memories of the brutality of the Nazi invasion, and the hardships of student life in Warsaw under the Occupation. But most of all this is a record of inward development; passages of remarkable intensity and simplicity

describe the girl's response to religion, to music, and to her discovery of philosophy.
Yolanthe Leigh was formerly a Lecturer in Philosophy at Reading University.
2000 • 56 pages • ISBN: 1-871551-46-3

Norman Cameron *by Warren Hope*
Norman Cameron's poetry was admired by W.H. Auden, celebrated by Dylan Thomas and valued by Robert Graves. He was described by Martin Seymour-Smith as, "one of … the most rewarding and pure poets of his generation …" and is at last given a full-length biography. This eminently sociable man, who had periods of darkness and despair, wrote little poetry by comparison with others of his time, but it is always of a consistently high quality – imaginative and profound.
2000 • 220 pages • illustrated • ISBN 1-871551-05-6

POETRY

Adam's Thoughts in Winter *by Warren Hope*
Warren Hope's poems have appeared from time to time in a number of literary periodicals, pamphlets and anthologies on both sides of the Atlantic. They appeal to lovers of poetry everywhere. His poems are brief, clear, frequently lyrical, characterised by wit, but often distinguished by tenderness. The poems gathered in this first book-length collection counter the brutalising ethos of contemporary life, speaking of, and for, the virtues of modesty, honesty and gentleness in an individual, memorable way.
2000 • 46 pages • ISBN 1-871551-40-4

Baudelaire: Les Fleurs du Mal *Translated by F.W. Leakey*
Selected poems from *Les Fleurs du Mal* are translated with parallel French texts and are designed to be read with pleasure by readers who have no French as well as those who are practised in the French language.
F.W. Leakey was Professor of French in the University of London. As a scholar, critic and teacher he specialised in the work of Baudelaire for 50 years and published a number of books on the poet.
2001 • 152 pages • ISBN 1-871551-10-2

'The Last Blackbird' and other poems by Ralph Hodgson *edited and introduced by John Harding*
Ralph Hodgson (1871-1962) was a poet and illustrator whose most influential and enduring work appeared to great acclaim just prior to, and during, the First World War. His work is imbued with a spiritual passion for the beauty of creation and the mystery of existence. This new selection

brings together, for the first time in 40 years, some of the most beautiful and powerful 'hymns to life' in the English language.
John Harding lives in London. He is a freelance writer and teacher and is Ralph Hodgson's biographer.
2004 • 70 pages • ISBN 1-871551-81-1

Lines from the Stone Age *by Sean Haldane*
Reviewing Sean Haldane's 1992 volume *Desire in Belfast*, Robert Nye wrote in *The Times* that "Haldane can be sure of his place among the English poets." This place is not yet a conspicuous one, mainly because his early volumes appeared in Canada, and because he has earned his living by other means than literature. Despite this, his poems have always had their circle of readers. The 60 previously unpublished poems of *Lines from the Stone Age* – "lines of longing, terror, pride, lust and pain" – may widen this circle.
2000 • 52 pages • ISBN 1-871551-39-0

Shakespeare's Sonnets *by Martin Seymour-Smith*
Martin Seymour-Smith's outstanding achievement lies in the field of literary biography and criticism. In 1963 he produced his comprehensive edition, in the old spelling, of *Shakespeare's Sonnets* (here revised and corrected by himself and Peter Davies in 1998). With its landmark introduction and its brilliant critical commentary on each sonnet, it was praised by William Empson and John Dover Wilson. Stephen Spender said of him "I greatly admire Martin Seymour-Smith for the independence of his views and the great interest of his mind"; and both Robert Graves and Anthony Burgess described him as the leading critic of his time. His exegesis of the *Sonnets* remains unsurpassed.
2001 • 194 pages • ISBN 1-871551-38-2

The Rain and the Glass *by Robert Nye*
When Robert Nye's first poems were published, G.S. Fraser declared in the *Times Literary Supplement*: "Here is a proper poet, though it is hard to see how the larger literary public (greedy for flattery of their own concerns) could be brought to recognize that. But other proper poets – how many of them are left? – will recognize one of themselves."
Since then Nye has become known to a large public for his novels, especially *Falstaff* (1976), winner of the Hawthornden Prize and The Guardian Fiction Prize, and *The Late Mr Shakespeare* (1998). But his true vocation has always been poetry, and it is as a poet that he is best known to his fellow poets. "Nye is the inheritor of a poetic tradition that runs from Donne and Ralegh to Edward Thomas and Robert Graves," wrote James Aitchison in 1990, while the critic Gabriel Josipovici has described him as "one of the most

interesting poets writing today, with a voice unlike that of any of his contemporaries".
This book contains all the poems Nye has written since his *Collected Poems* of 1995, together with his own selection from that volume. An introduction, telling the story of his poetic beginnings, affirms Nye's unfashionable belief in inspiration, as well as defining that quality of unforced truth which distinguishes the best of his work: "I have spent my life trying to write poems, but the poems gathered here came mostly when I was not."
2005 • 132 pages • ISBN 1-871551-41-2

Wilderness *by Martin Seymour-Smith*
This is Martin Seymour-Smith's first publication of his poetry for more than twenty years. This collection of 36 poems is a fearless account of an inner life of love, frustration, guilt, laughter and the celebration of others. He is best known to the general public as the author of the controversial and bestselling *Hardy* (1994).
1994 • 52 pages • ISBN 1-871551-08-0

BUSINESS

English Language Skills *by Vera Hughes*
If you want to be sure, (as a student, or in your business or personal life), that your written English is correct, this book is for you. Vera Hughes' aim is to help you to remember the basic rules of spelling, grammar and punctuation. 'Noun', 'verb', 'subject', 'object' and 'adjective' are the only technical terms used. The book teaches the clear, accurate English required by the business and office world. It coaches acceptable current usage and makes the rules easier to remember.
Vera Hughes was a civil servant and is a trainer and author of training manuals.
2002 • 142 pages • ISBN 1-871551-60-9

The Essential Accounting Dictionary of Key Financial Terms
by Linda Hodgson
This is a key aide for students seeking examination success in Accounting A-Level and GNVQ Advanced Business. It results from work with teachers and students and addresses common difficulties. Straightforward, easy to read definitions of key financial terms – which form the basis of understanding and better performance at tests and examination. There is a multiple choice quiz to crosscheck how much the student knows.
Linda Jane Hodgson, graduate in History and Politics, is a former Tax

Inspector and qualified teacher. Professionally, she also advised accounting firms on taxation. She now teaches business and finance at a London college.
1999 • 150 pages • ISBN 1-871551-50-1